Nuclear Weapons Policy at the Crossroads

Darryl Howlett, Tanya Ogilvie-White,
John Simpson and Emily Taylor

DATE DUE

Published in Great Britain in 2000
by the Royal Institute of International Affairs,
Chatham House, 10 St James's Square, London SW1Y 4LE
(Charity Registration No. 208 223)

Distributed worldwide by the Brookings Institution,
1775 Massachusetts Avenue, NW, Washington, DC 20036-2188

ISBN 1 86203 110 X

Cover design by Matthew Link
Printed and bound in Great Britain by the Chameleon Press Ltd

*The Royal Institute of International Affairs is an independent body which
promotes the rigorous study of international questions and does not express
opinions of its own. The opinions expressed in this publication are the
responsibility of the authors.*

*The Mountbatten Centre for International Studies is a research centre in
the Department of Politics at the University of Southampton specializing in
multilateral security issues.*

CONTENTS

ABOUT THE AUTHORS

Dr Darryl Howlett is a Senior Lecturer in International Relations in the Department of Politics, University of Southampton.

Dr Tanya Ogilvie-White is a visiting fellow in the Mountbatten Centre for International Studies, Department of Politics, University of Southampton.

Professor John Simpson is Director of the Mountbatten Centre for International Studies and Programme Director of the Programme for Promoting Nuclear Non-Proliferation (PPNN).

Emily Taylor is Projects Manager for the Mountbatten Centre for International Studies and Programme Coordinator of the PPNN.

ACKNOWLEDGMENTS

The contents of this publication are the sole responsibility of its authors. However, we would like to acknowledge the input of those who also wrote or contributed to the working papers that provided the basis for this study: Roy Allison, Wyn Q. Bowen, Ben Cole, Camille Grand, Nadine Gurr, Richard Guthrie, Peter Jones, Ian Kenyon, Lawrence Scheinman, and Michael Yahuda.

Additional thanks go to those who attended the four Validation Meetings held between 1996 and 2000 and commented on the work in progress. The study also draws on the literature presented in the bibliography and on interviews and other meetings that the contributors have conducted and attended during the course of the research.

Special thanks are also due to Angela Woodward, Lucy Smith and Angela Murphy at the Mountbatten Centre for International Studies, and to William Hopkinson and Margaret May at the Royal Institute of International Affairs.

May 2000   D.H.
                                                             T.O.-W.
                                                               J.S.
                                                               E.T.

PREFACE

This study on nuclear futures is a product of work undertaken by the Mountbatten Centre for International Studies (MCIS) of the University of Southampton. The study has pursued three goals: to attempt to understand the dynamics of the nuclear present; to elucidate a range of possible nuclear futures that may emerge; and to assess different strategies that could be pursued in response to these futures, including proposals for promoting nuclear disarmament. The aim was to draw on research, meetings and outreach to achieve these goals, and to use the knowledge gained to help inform the international policy-making community.

The study began in 1996 at a time when the end of the Cold War was widely believed to have opened a window of opportunity for movement towards a nuclear-weapon-free world (NWFW). There were good reasons for this optimism. The emergence of new global, political, economic and security structures had led the Western nuclear-weapon states (NWS) to reassess the nature of the security challenges they faced and the military capabilities required to meet them. Concerns about the financial and political costs of sustaining existing nuclear-weapons systems were becoming more important and fears over the environmental hazards posed by weapons of mass destruction (WMD) were attracting more attention. As a result of these factors, significant reductions were made in both the composition and the deployment of the nuclear armaments of the Western allies, and a number of non-nuclear-weapon states (NNWS) began reassessing their own commitment to extended nuclear deterrence.

These developments appeared to represent a dramatic break with the nuclear world of the period from 1945 to 1989 when nuclear weapons played a prominent role both in strategic thinking and in the East–West context. However, as the work progressed, regional and global proliferation dynamics, international political tensions and serious difficulties in arms control negotiations indicated that the break with the nuclear past might not be permanent. A view emerged that suggested the window of opportunity was already closing and that progress in disarmament was beginning to reverse. Fears over the proliferation of WMD in the Middle East, South Asia and Northeast Asia, and the potential for a new offence–defence arms race between the NWS, began to undermine the confidence of nuclear policy-makers and strategic analysts, and provoked greater uncertainty over what the future held. These factors added another dimension to the study: an assessment of the conditions that could lead to a future where nuclear weapons again occupy a prominent role in international relations and an examination of the likely characteristics of such a future.

The study has utilized the extensive non-proliferation literature within the public domain, as well as the work of academic consultants with specialist knowledge of the nuclear debate and of individuals who have worked within relevant policy-making circles. It should be noted, however, that the vast majority of the available sources were of European or American origin. This has important implications for the material used in writing this study and the conclusions it has reached, in that they are unavoidably based on Western perspectives.

The work underlying this study was divided into two stages. During the first stage, the apparent threat perceptions of the five acknowledged NWS (China, France, Russia, the UK and the United States) and the three *de facto* NWS (India, Israel and Pakistan) were explored. The purpose of this research was to identify the main factors (or shapers) that seem to have influenced nuclear weapons policy in all these states, and to assess their relative importance.

The second stage of the work drew on the conclusions reached on the eight countries. The shapers were divided into categories on the basis of their apparent impact on nuclear weapons policy. Strategic relationships, military factors and developments in technology were considered to be 'first-order shapers'. These had already been dealt with in the papers on threat perceptions. Domestic considerations, changing conceptions of security and arms control initiatives were labelled 'second-order shapers' because they appeared to be becoming more influential, but their impact was dependent on changes in the strategic environment (i.e. on the first-order shapers). The final category of shapers, which encompassed verification methods, issues of compliance and disarmament strategies, were labelled 'third-order shapers'. This was because their impact on nuclear weapons policy was considered to be less influential, but they were likely to be crucial if a NWFW was to come within reach.[1]

This study summarizes the main conclusions reached in the course of this work. It is divided into three parts. The first analyses the nature of the three categories of shapers and their impact on nuclear weapons policy. It also assesses how the balance between these shapers could change over the next 20 to 30 years and the conditions that would be necessary for this transition. The second part elucidates three nuclear futures that could emerge over the next two to three decades, depending on how the shapers evolve: a high-salience nuclear future; a lower-salience nuclear future; and a NWFW. The third part addresses the strengths and weaknesses of the instruments and strategies that could be pursued in order to promote stability and security in the future nuclear environment.

---

[1] Of the five NWS and the three *de facto* NWS, the US plays the most significant role in shaping nuclear decision-making – US strategic relationships, threat perceptions, and technological advances have a strong influence on the nuclear environment. The same can be argued where second- and third-order shapers are concerned, as the US domestic nuclear debate and US attitudes to verification, compliance and disarmament have uniquely widespread repercussions. Ideally, a model would have been developed that reflected this phenomenon, as well as the relative influence of the remaining seven states, but it was felt that this would have unduly complicated the project's framework for analysis. Nevertheless, it is worth emphasizing the disproportionate impact of the US on the nuclear environment.

ABBREVIATIONS

ABM	Anti-Ballistic Missile (Treaty)
ALCM	Air-Launched Cruise Missile
BJP	Bharatiya Janata Party
BMD	Ballistic Missile Defence
BTWC	Bacteriological and Toxins Weapons Convention
BW	Biological Weapons
CD	Conference on Disarmament
CFE	Conventional Forces in Europe (Treaty)
CMC	Computer Malicious Code
CTBT	Comprehensive Test-Ban Treaty
CW	Chemical Weapons
CWC	Chemical Weapons Convention
DoD	Department of Defense (US)
DPRK	Democratic People's Republic of Korea
EU	European Union
FMCT	Fissile Material Cut-off Treaty
FRY	Federal Republic of Yugoslavia
HE	High-Explosive
IAEA	International Atomic Energy Agency
ICBM	Intercontinental Ballistic Missile
IGMDP	Integrated Guided Missile Development Plan
INF	Intermediate-Range Nuclear Forces
MCIS	Mountbatten Centre for International Studies
MEADS	Medium Extended Air Defence System
MIRV	Multiple Independently Targetable Re-entry Vehicle
MOX	Mixed Oxide (Fuel)
MTCR	Missile Technology Control Regime
NAC	New Agenda Coalition
NART	Nuclear Arms Reduction Treaty

NATO	North Atlantic Treaty Organization
NBC	Nuclear, Biological or Chemical
NGO	Non-Governmental Organization
NMD	National Missile Defence
NNWS	Non-Nuclear-Weapon States
NPG	Nuclear Planning Group
NPR	Nuclear Posture Review
NPT	Non-Proliferation Treaty
NWFW	Nuclear-Weapon-Free World
NWFZ	Nuclear-Weapon-Free Zone
NWS	Nuclear-Weapon States
OPCW	Organization for the Prohibition of Chemical Weapons
P5	Five Permanent Members of the UN Security Council
R&D	Research and Development
RMA	Revolution in Military Affairs
ROK	Republic of Korea
SLBM	Submarine-Launched Ballistic Missile
SSBN	Nuclear Powered Ballistic Missile Submarine
START	Strategic Arms Reduction Treaty
TMD	Theatre Missile Defence
VNA	Virtual Nuclear Arsenal
WEU	Western European Union
WMD	Weapons of Mass Destruction
ZFWMD	Zone Free of Weapons of Mass Destruction

PART I

THE SHAPERS OF NUCLEAR POLICY

THE NUCLEAR PRESENT

A brief overview of the nuclear postures and doctrines of the nuclear-weapon states and the *de facto* NWS will provide an introduction to the nuclear present. It shows that although the end of the Cold War has witnessed a spate of reductions in nuclear weaponry, conceptions of nuclear deterrence, and of the role and utility of nuclear weapons remain core elements in national security policies

In the 1994 Nuclear Posture Review (NPR), US policy-makers concluded that for the foreseeable future their country should continue to rely on nuclear weapons and deterrence for its security needs. In the short term at least, the US decided to maintain its triad of nuclear forces at the levels agreed under START II in order to deter Russia, China and other potentially hostile states from using nuclear weapons. There was also some speculation over whether the US was developing new, low-yield nuclear weapons for use in a surgical strike role as part of the so-called Counter-Proliferation Initiative. Although some experts doubted this development, others believed that such an initiative might be intended to enhance the defensive capability of the US and its allies in the face of perceived threats from hostile states with nuclear and/or biological weapons and advanced delivery capabilities.

Russia's 1993 Military Doctrine reaffirmed its belief in the deterrent value of its nuclear arsenal. Military expenditure had dropped drastically since the end of the Cold War, but all the signs indicated that Russia was more committed than ever to the retention of its nuclear capabilities. This was confirmed in May 1997 by high-ranking Russian officials who claimed that the strategic nuclear forces formed the 'backbone' of Russia's defence and that this force should be bolstered to maintain Russia's international status. Additionally, on 10 January 2000, Russia adopted a new National Security Concept that placed greater emphasis on external threats, and on the role of nuclear weapons for deterrent purposes and for their use 'in the event of the need to repulse armed aggression, if all other measures of resolving the crisis situation have been exhausted and have proved ineffective'.

China's armed forces were believed to have undertaken a major review of their nuclear capabilities and doctrine at the end of the Cold War, resulting in the implementation of an extensive force modernization programme and the adoption of a revised strategic doctrine, known as limited deterrence. Although there is little information in the open literature about China's modernization programme, the new strategic doctrine suggested that Beijing would be focusing on qualitative developments. These might include the development of more accurate intercontinental ballistic missiles (ICBMs); the modernization of air and sea delivery vehicles; the introduction of technologies that would improve the penetrability of warheads in the face of space- and ground-based ballistic missile defence (BMD); the development of nuclear-armed anti-satellite systems;

and the creation of the necessary command, control, communication, computer and intelligence systems for directing nuclear forces at different levels of confrontation.[2] Such a programme would require massive investment and be indicative of a long-term commitment on the part of the Chinese government to nuclear ordnance.

Recent French security policy has been characterized by a lower reliance on nuclear weapons than during the Cold War. Military spending has declined by more than one-third since 1991. However, this does not indicate that France plans to move to zero. Since the end of the Cold War, no French policy-maker or official document has criticized or challenged the role of nuclear weapons in French security policy. Although the 1994 White Paper put new emphasis on conventional forces and pointed to a reduced role for nuclear weapons in French strategy, the French conception of nuclear deterrence was reaffirmed. According to this White Paper, the nuclear forces must be capable of fulfilling two functions: first, 'to inflict a striking force causing unacceptable damage and liable to be repeated'; and, second, 'to proceed to a limited striking force on military targets in view of the ultimate warning' [official translation].

Since 1991, the UK has been engaged in a policy of structural change to its nuclear forces and posture. A submarine-based nuclear missile force has been retained, with its missiles supplied by the US and with joint targeting arrangements involving that state, but the remainder of the UK's pre–1991 nuclear capability has been

[2] For commentary, see for example Alastair Iain Johnston, 'China's New "Old Thinking": The Concept of Limited Deterrence', *International Security*, Vol. 20, No. 3, Winter 1995–96, pp. 5–42.

retired. The diverse basing modes, delivery systems and warhead types of the Cold War period have been replaced by the Trident delivery system alone. In the UK's 1998 Strategic Defence Review, it was stated that this system was to have an inventory of nuclear warheads that will not exceed 200, although the basis for the nuclear policy remains essentially unchanged as a deterrent role for nuclear weapons is still envisaged.

Until recently, both India and Pakistan were firmly committed to the notion of nuclear ambiguity or opaqueness. Both states signalled that they possessed the capability to produce nuclear weapons at short notice and the means to deliver them, but neither was prepared to be seen to have developed, or be in possession of, an overt nuclear deterrent. Developments in 1998 and 1999 suggested that this situation has changed, as both states engaged in a series of nuclear tests followed by highly publicized missile launches. Also, on 17 August 1999, India released a draft nuclear doctrine outlining its plans to pursue a policy of credible minimum nuclear deterrence and stating that 'any nuclear attack on India and its forces shall result in punitive retaliation with nuclear weapons to inflict damage unacceptable to the aggressor'. These actions, combined with the public statements emanating from India and Pakistan about inducting nuclear weapons into their armed forces, suggested that both states may now be contemplating weaponization and deployment.

Since the end of the Cold War, Israel has become more explicit about its nuclear strategy and doctrine. The size of Israel's nuclear arsenal remains a closely guarded secret, but in 1995 Israel, for the first time, indicated its commitment to, and dependence on, its nuclear capability. This position is unlikely to change for the foreseeable future. Successive governments have appeared reluctant to engage in substantive arms control initiatives, including the creation of zones free of weapons of mass destruction (ZFWMD), until a lasting peace settlement is achieved in the Middle East. However, Israel has been under pressure from the US to support negotiations on a global halt to the production of weapons-grade fissile materials to move forward at the Conference on Disarmament (CD) in Geneva.

Introduction

One assumption of this study is that strategic relationships between the NWS and the *de facto* NWS, together with military and technological developments within these states, are currently the primary shapers of nuclear weapons policy. Since the end of the Cold War, other shapers have gained momentum, but traditional concerns over military threats and political disputes have re-emerged and continue to dominate the nuclear debate. If this situation continues, further progress in nuclear arms reductions will, at best, be slow and limited; at worst, the world could experience a round of arms competition, with unknown consequences.

Key strategic relationships

The trend towards improved strategic relations between the NWS appears to be faltering. At the end of the Cold

War, the warming of relations between the US and Russia created the necessary momentum to move co-operative negotiations over nuclear reductions forward. More recently, conflicts of interest between Moscow and Washington involving NATO expansion, US policy towards Iraq and NATO action against the Federal Republic of Yugoslavia (FRY) have caused this process to flounder. This has undermined the confidence of both states in their developing relationship and has led to complications in furthering the START process.

US and Russian nuclear policies are crucially affected by the two countries' mutual relationship. For the US, Russia is still the most significant state in its strategic calculus because of Moscow's continued deployment of nuclear forces that can target the US mainland. Officials in Washington are particularly concerned about the potential consequences were Russian democracy to collapse. Such a situation could lead to renewed nuclear challenges, higher defence budgets, spreading instability, the loss of new markets and a devastating setback for the worldwide democratic movement. If the democratization process continues to evolve following the election of President Putin, then the prospects for a productive partnership and nuclear reductions are propitious. Conversely, if this process falters, renewed discord may ensue.

Relations between the old Cold War adversaries and China have been equally complex. Although neither the US nor China seeks confrontation, there has been a marked deterioration in relations between the two states since the mid-1990s. The crisis over Taiwan in 1995–6 was the most important contributory factor. But added to this, the recent allegations of Chinese infiltration of US nuclear facilities and the NATO action against the FRY in 1999, during which the Chinese embassy in Belgrade was hit, have also increased mutual distrust and animosity. Given that the US and China openly identify each other as a potential major threat and as one of the primary motivations to maintain and develop their respective nuclear weapons programmes, it is fair to surmise that further deterioration of relations between Beijing and Washington will reinforce their commitment to nuclear weaponry.

There is some concern that NATO's adoption of a new Strategic Concept in April 1999 may exacerbate tensions between the Western NWS and their rivals. Although the NATO allies have stressed their joint commitment to 'consider options' for arms control and disarmament, the new concept is seen as destabilizing, and even threatening, by both China and Russia. Concerns appear to stem from interpretations of paragraphs 64 and 65 of the Washington Summit Communiqué. Paragraph 64 states that NATO's 'ability to defuse a crisis through diplomatic and other means or, should it be necessary, to mount a successful conventional defence has significantly improved'. Paragraph 65 refers to a 'transformed NATO', which is able to 'contribute to the evolving security environment, supporting security and stability with the strength of its shared commitment to democracy and the peaceful resolution of disputes'. Russia regards this document as evidence that NATO is undergoing a transformation from a defensive to an offensive body with a global mission, operating outside the framework of the United Nations Security Council. NATO action against the FRY was viewed by Moscow as confirmation of this development and may have reinforced Russia's determination to maintain and even upgrade its nuclear arsenal despite any economic constraints. Russia's announcement in May 1999 that it will carry out, 'as a matter of priority', five underground subcritical nuclear tests at the Novaya Zemlya test site could be seen as a response to NATO's new Strategic Concept. The tests are thought to stem from a decision to upgrade Moscow's tactical nuclear forces.

At present, relations between Russia and China are improving. The most likely effects of this will be to increase US determination to maintain strategic superiority, rather than to increase the incentives for Beijing and Moscow to downgrade their nuclear arsenals. At the 1996 Beijing Summit, Russia and China declared their 'strategic partnership for the next century'. Despite these signs of a more enduring cooperative partnership, this relationship is fraught with historical tensions that are unlikely to be forgotten. However, the opposition of China and Russia to perceived US hegemony and to NATO's evolving role may encourage greater political and economic cooperation between these two traditional rivals. If this were to include a nuclear dimension, it could undermine Western aspirations to further arms control and non-proliferation objectives.

During the Cold War, and especially after France left NATO's integrated military organization, there was little formal contact between London and Paris over nuclear security questions. Since 1991, however, cooperation between the UK and France over all aspects of military activities, and in particular nuclear policy, has intensified. This cooperation initially assisted in persuading France that the way forward was reintegration into NATO and opened up the possibility of discussing the European role of French nuclear forces in the NATO Nuclear Planning Group (NPG), rather than in the context of the EU and the Western European Union (WEU). Later, these closer ties also enabled the UK to accept development of a more prominent role for a security policy in the EU.

The only strategic relationship that could have an immediate impact on Israel's nuclear policies is its strategic partnership with the US. If this relationship were to deteriorate, it must be assumed that Israel's nuclear posture would become more assertive. However, while there has been suggestion of a slight weakening in the US commitment to Israel since the early 1990s, bilateral relations remain strong. Improved relations between Israel and its Cold War opponents, Russia and China, are also likely to have longer-term effects. Since the end of the Cold War, both Moscow and Beijing have re-established diplomatic links with Tel Aviv and have demonstrated their support for peace and stability in the Middle East. This has bolstered the peace process and is likely to bring the possibility of negotiations over the nuclear issue a step closer.

Changes in the strategic environment since the end of the Cold War have had destabilizing effects in South Asia. This has increased insecurity in India and Pakistan, encouraging both states to engage in nuclear testing and possible weaponization. A major factor has been the deterioration of the US–Pakistan 'special relationship'. This has strengthened Pakistan's pro-weapons advocates, who have argued that the acquisition of nuclear weapons is the only guarantee of stability in a situation where military independence has been forced upon Islamabad by US domestic legislation. This situation has been exacerbated by reports that India and Russia have been engaged in negotiations over the transfer of sophisticated military technology, including advanced air-defence missiles, and that China has assisted Pakistan's nuclear weapon and missile programmes. Policy-makers in New Delhi have argued that the transfer of technology from China to Pakistan is the more significant of the two activities, and poses a greater threat to regional stability. They have also cited the possession of nuclear weapons by China, and the threats to their country arising from this, as a direct motivation for their own nuclear activities. The intense insecurity created by this uncertain strategic environment has had a major impact on the nuclear policies of both states. Since the end of the Cold War, regional tensions have escalated, long-running disputes in Kashmir, Assam and Punjab have been inflamed, and support for nuclear weapons has increased.

Military threats

During the Cold War, the threat of direct and imminent nuclear attack by the US or the Soviet Union was the most influential factor shaping the nuclear policies of the NWS. Now that relations between the Cold War rivals have improved in relative terms, these dynamics are somewhat diminished. However, new perceived military threats are emerging, including the possibility of nuclear, biological or chemical (NBC) attack by states wishing to challenge the status quo. These threats have expanded the scope of the NWS deterrence doctrines, and increased the incentives to explore the costs and benefits of developing more sophisticated conventional weapons and missile defence systems.

At present, traditional modes of thinking dominate debates on the role of nuclear weapons, especially where the subject of deterrence is concerned. One outcome of this is that some analysts have inferred a general principle from Europe's experience after the Second World War that nuclear deterrence can aid in the prevention of war and induce future peace and stability. In contrast, others have noted three aspects of the contemporary situation which indicate that a reassessment of this principle may be required. First, it has been questioned whether nuclear ordnance has a role to play in deterring the biological and advanced conventional weapons of the present and future. Second, the existence of competing conceptions of deterrence (from the various forms of overt deterrence of the NWS to the opaque deterrence of Israel and the ambiguous deterrence of the Democratic People's Republic of Korea (DPRK)), may make nuclear behaviour less predictable and therefore create more opportunities for dangerous misunderstandings between nuclear adversaries. Third, the huge range of capabilities that exists among the NWS, the *de facto* NWS and any

11

aspiring nuclear-weapon states may undermine the credibility of nuclear deterrence and thus increase the chances of nuclear war. Despite these doubts and calls for new thinking, there remains a tendency to seek solutions derived from traditional ideas about deterrence in tackling these emerging threats.

The US now considers the proliferation of WMD to be one of the principal threats to its security. Initially, its policy focus was on containing the potential for nuclear proliferation arising from the dissolution of the Soviet Union. In an attempt to prevent this, the states left with former Soviet nuclear weaponry on their territory (Belarus, Kazakhstan and Ukraine) were offered incentives to transfer their inherited arsenals to Russia. The success of this scheme allayed the immediate proliferation concerns of Western policy-makers, but the political, economic and social instability in Russia continues to provoke unease about how effectively the central government could guard and account for its stocks of WMD and materials. To this have been added the modernization of China's limited nuclear arsenal, the proliferation of WMD to states hostile to US interests, and the potential for terrorist use of WMD.

During the 1990s, following the end of the East–West confrontation, both France and the UK undertook a reassessment of their respective security policies. The former's 1994 White Paper stated that 'for the first time in history, France does not face a direct military threat near its borders'. This helps explain the French decision to dismantle 18 surface-to-surface medium-range strategic missiles, which until 1996 had been on permanent alert on the Albion Plateau in central France. These installations, which were set up by President de Gaulle in the 1960s to bring targets in the Soviet Union within range, were no longer seen as necessary. However, the White Paper did identify the existence of a potential indirect military threat should France become involved overseas against a regional adversary armed with WMD. The document also highlighted the risks and uncertainties surrounding developments in Russia, and showed a growing concern over Chinese nuclear policy. As a result, the French conception of nuclear deterrence was reaffirmed.

Among the potential future 'risks and challenges' identified by the UK in governmental reports and statements, attention has been paid to the problems posed by the spread of WMD and ballistic missiles. In particular, concern has been expressed over how to respond to a future adversary which is not allied to a NWS but has a potential nuclear capability, and how to respond to a chemical or biological threat from such a state. However, the main concerns of UK policy-makers relate to Russia's residual nuclear capability and the uncertainties arising from the collapse of the former Soviet Union, and any modernization of China's nuclear systems which might give it a global reach.

The Washington Summit Communiqué identified the proliferation of WMD as a 'matter of serious concern' for NATO and outlined the 'WMD Initiative' as the Alliance's response to this threat. This initiative is intended to coordinate the Allies' non-proliferation efforts and 'increase military readiness to operate in a

WMD environment and to counter WMD threats'. According to the new Strategic Concept, these efforts include the maintenance of an effective nuclear deterrent force in Europe to 'prevent coercion'. This assigns a significant military and political role to nuclear weapons within NATO and shows that, although the Alliance has stressed 'the reduced salience of nuclear weapons' in the post-Cold War strategic environment, NATO believes that such weapons will continue to play a pivotal deterrent role in maintaining peace and security.

The Russian National Security Concept 2000 identified the proliferation of WMD and their delivery systems as one of its principal sources of external danger. Indeed, Russia's geographical proximity to the *de facto* NWS and possibly any nuclear aspirant states means that these states will be capable of posing a threat to Russia sooner than they will to the US, France or the UK. Iran could be viewed by Moscow as posing an imminent threat to Russia through its development of the Shihab–3 and Shihab–4 systems, which would be capable of targeting small parts of southern Russia and large parts of Central Asia, where Iran has strategic interests. There is uncertainty over how India and Pakistan might interact with Russia in a crisis over Central Asia. Policy-makers in Moscow may also be concerned about nuclear developments in the DPRK, which is capable of striking limited parts of the Russian Far East.

Since the end of the Cold War, the residual nuclear forces of the US, and those of other NWS, the *de facto* NWS and any nuclear aspirant states, have played an important role in the decision of Russia to rely on its nuclear forces as the 'backbone' of its defence. However, of equal significance has been the threat posed by a major conventional attack, which its conventional armed forces might be incapable of repelling. In spite of its recent ratifications of START II and the Comprehensive Test Ban Treaty (CTBT), Russia is relying on its nuclear forces to deter both WMD and conventional threats to its security, and is likely to do so for the foreseeable future unless it makes unexpected economic progress. Thus, although the salience of nuclear weapons appears to be declining in the West, this is not the case in Russia. The details of Russia's new military doctrine, published in October 1999, reinforced this argument.

Beijing's decision to implement a force modernization programme may have been driven by an awareness of its technological inferiority relative to the US and Russian nuclear weapons programmes. While the emphasis has been on improving diplomatic relations with Washington and Moscow, Beijing remains deeply distrustful of US global 'hegemony' and Russian territorial ambitions, and appears to be seeking the capability to reciprocate if either state threatens China with a NBC attack. The desire to make qualitative improvements to its nuclear arsenal may also have been motivated by fear both of future development of WMD in Taiwan and Japan and of any deployment of Theatre Missile Defence (TMD) systems in either territory. Although China may not currently face an adversary armed with an indigenous nuclear arsenal in Northeast Asia, any deterioration of US strategic partnerships with China's traditional rivals could spark a regional nuclear arms race. This could explain China's willingness to take part in negotiations to remove the nuclear threat from the DPRK, which is also seen by Beijing as a potential shaper of nuclear proliferation in Japan and Taiwan.

Threats posed by WMD are currently the primary shaper of nuclear policy in the *de facto* NWS. China's defence modernization programme and Pakistan's nuclear weapons programme have been the cause of great unease in India, leading the New Delhi government to push ahead with its missile and space programmes. Pakistan has responded to these developments by trying to demonstrate that it is able to match India's capabilities with its own missile tests. The mutual feelings of vulnerability generated by these activities have now escalated to a point where both countries have been undergoing a major reassessment of their nuclear policies. In 1998 India and Pakistan both conducted a series of nuclear and missile tests to demonstrate their nuclear ordnance and delivery capabilities. This was followed in August 1999 by the release of a draft policy document by India outlining a doctrine of minimum deterrence based on a triad of nuclear forces.

The threat of attack by WMD has long been a crucial shaper of Israel's nuclear policies. Such threat percep-tions have multiplied since the end of the Cold War and the 1991 Gulf War. In March 1995, Prime Minister Peres articulated Israel's fears, stating that 'Israel is the only country in the world that another country is threatening to destroy physically, militarily, and otherwise. Not only are they threatening, they are trying to get a nuclear option and missiles to do so.' Iraq's Scud attacks on Israeli civilians in 1991, as well as reports of Iraq's WMD capabilities and Iran's nuclear development, have brought these concerns into sharp focus.

Developments in technology

It is difficult to anticipate what impact developments in nuclear and conventional weapons technologies will have on the nuclear policies of the NWS and the *de facto* NWS. On the one hand, it is possible that the revolution in military affairs (RMA) and developments in missile defence systems could reduce the role of nuclear ordnance, undermine conceptions of nuclear deterrence and thus weaken the incentives to maintain nuclear weapons programmes. On the other hand, it is equally possible that such developments could generate pressures to acquire a new range of nuclear weapons and their delivery systems, provoke a new offence–defence nuclear arms race between the NWS, and also encourage greater interest in biological weapons programmes. The most likely outcome may fall somewhere between these two extremes: a differentiated or asymmetrical situation of reduced reliance on nuclear ordnance for states with the economic and technological capability to exploit the RMA, coupled with increased reliance on WMD by states lacking such capabilities.

The RMA and nuclear weapon policies

The most significant element of the RMA for nuclear weaponry has been the revolution in guidance systems. Small facilities can now be located by technical surveillance and computerized intelligence and targeted by a precision-guided high-explosive (HE) weapon. Aircraft shelters hardened to withstand huge overpressures have become vulnerable to direct-hit HE bombs guided either by laser or by the Global Positioning Satellite system. Hand-launched missiles find their own way directly to tanks or aircraft. Remote targets need not be seen but can be located by technical surveillance, and a cruise missile can be launched to hit them. Further technical developments in guidance systems are likely, including ballistic missile terminal guidance, stealth or supersonic cruise missiles, and fast-response bad-weather surveillance. These developments could permit precise attacks against time-critical targets, including mobile missile launchers, command bunkers, and air and missile defence warning systems. They would also give military leaders options other than the use of wide-area weapons leading to massive destruction of populations, even in large-scale wars.

Assessments of the costs and opportunities of the RMA differ within and between states. Among the NWS and the *de facto* NWS, the US, Russia, Israel and India are showing the greatest interest in the potential benefits of advanced conventional weaponry. The general consensus in the US is that these new technologies will demand a reassessment of how the US military establishment operates in the future. Several studies have been undertaken in Washington to determine in what ways new technologies can be integrated into the US force posture. Similar studies are under way in Israel, where the military establishment is keen to develop precision-guided munitions and sophisticated command and control systems for a 'slimmer and smarter' force. Strategic analysts in Russia and India are also arguing that the deterrence role of nuclear weapons can be replicated by more effective conventional systems, but both states are likely to be constrained by economic considerations from exploiting such systems for the foreseeable future. Russia, for one, has displayed an interest in trading constraints on such weapons in return for limitations on its own non-strategic nuclear capabilities.

Analysts in China, France and the UK appear more sceptical than their US counterparts about the alleged revolutionary impact of the RMA. Although the published research in China indicates considerable interest, the country's leaders do not appear to view the development of these systems as an alternative to nuclear weapons. A similar assessment appears to have been made by the French military: the 1994 White Paper described 'theories of conventional deterrence' as 'dangerous mistakes'. Policy-makers in the UK, while evincing interest in the future role of information technology in warfare, also continue to believe that nuclear deterrence represents the most appropriate and cost-effective means for preventing war.

Despite the scepticism of some states, conventional weaponry may come to eclipse the role of nuclear weapons in states with the financial and technological ability to develop them. There are already indications that this process is beginning. However, even the US military has a long way to advance in the field of conventional 'precision strike' before it will seriously consider a significant shift in its strategic forces away from nuclear weapons towards a greater reliance on advanced conventional weaponry. But this has not allayed the fears of states that are concerned about the prospect of being left behind in the race for such weapons, including Russia and China. Russia's political and military leaders have made no secret of their insecurities in this regard, or of their resultant feelings of dependency on nuclear ordnance. Such feelings appear to have intensified following NATO's use of advanced conventional weaponry during the Kosovo war.

While the RMA may be starting to reduce the salience of nuclear weapons in the most technologically and economically advanced states, this is by no means universal, and will not necessarily have the effect of encouraging moves towards a NWFW. Indeed, the RMA could have the opposite effect if WMD are seen as an effective response to these new conventional weapons. Whereas nuclear weapons have tended to be the weapons of choice of the most powerful states and militaries, they may in future become the preferred instruments for deterrence or compellence by the weaker against the stronger. Nuclear weapons and missile delivery systems may be attractive to regional states, which are not capable of developing precision-guided conventional weapons but seek to deter US, or allied, intervention to thwart their attempts at regional dominance. Moreover, if the technique of boosting to enhance the efficiency and reliability of fission weapons proves to be as straightforward as some have argued, it could encourage moves to venture down the nuclear path by offering an easier route to the development and deployment of nuclear ordnance.

It is also possible that the RMA may have the effect of increasing the incentives of weaker states to develop other forms of WMD and/or engage in information warfare. States that lack the financial capacity and technological know-how to develop nuclear weapons, or high-tech conventional weaponry, may choose to develop biological weapons. These are easier than nuclear ordnance to make, deliver and use subversively, and harder to detect and control through facility surveillance. For these reasons, they are also more likely to appeal to non-state actors, including terrorists. Such actors may also engage in information warfare against the most technologically advanced states. In particular, computer malicious codes (CMCs), designed to cause chaos when inserted into undefended links in computer networks, may be relatively cheap to produce and could be used to hold to ransom the military and civilian information infrastructures of advanced countries.

The development of ballistic missile defences (BMD)

The resumption of the debate over BMD in the US has been triggered by fears over the proliferation of WMD and the potential medium- and long-range missile threats from China and allegedly 'rogue' states such as the DPRK. Washington's policy-makers have therefore been assessing the advantages of developing a national missile defence (NMD) system against the disadvantages of threatening the sanctity of the Anti-Ballistic Missile (ABM) Treaty. Under the National Missile Defense Act of 1999, Congress authorized budget expenditure of $10.5 billion between 1999 and 2005 for the development of a limited NMD system. At the same time, the US announced steps to advance its TMD programme to protect US troops and allies from short- and medium-range missile threats. The decision over whether or not to deploy the NMD system will be made in summer 2000, and will be based on an assessment of whether it can be made operationally effective. As yet, the technological and scientific feasibility of the system remains unproven, but the US Department of Defense (DoD) hopes that a series of practical tests, which began in autumn 1999, will demonstrate that a workable NMD system can and should be built. The DoD is also said to hope that the first units of the system can be deployed in five years, although the Director for Defense Research and Engineering at the Pentagon has cited 2008–10 as the probable earliest period for deployment.

Some defence analysts in Washington have argued that the proposed US NMD would have limited capability against ICBM penetration measures, or against short-range cruise or ballistic missiles fired from merchant ships near US shores, but this has not stopped Russia from expressing acute concern over its implications. The Clinton administration has gone to great lengths to assuage these concerns. Secretary of Defense William Cohen has stressed that the NMD programme is focused primarily on countering threats from 'rogue' states and will not be capable of countering Russia's nuclear deterrent. However, Russia does not appear to be convinced and is concerned that incremental development of the NMD system would ultimately give the US the ability to counter strategic missiles, a capability that Russia itself is unlikely to be able to develop because of economic constraints. The Russian foreign ministry has accused the US of challenging strategic stability and international security, arguing that US deployment of NMD would stimulate the deployment of more sophisticated missiles, trigger a new arms race and undermine the whole disarmament process. Consequently, there is concern that without agreement on amendments to the ABM Treaty Russia will embark on a programme to modernize its offensive strategic nuclear weapon systems.

China is also highly sensitive about the issue of BMD because such systems are likely to degrade its limited deterrent capability. China's greatest concern is likely to be US TMD research and development cooperation with, or actual TMD deployments to, states around its periphery. First, TMD assistance to Taiwan would be viewed as threatening both because improvements in Taiwan's military capabilities could encourage further moves towards independence and because TMD systems would blunt one of the few military instruments Beijing has to pressure Taiwan, conventionally armed ballistic missiles. Second, US TMD cooperation or deployments to Japan might also appear threatening because many Chinese leaders still view Japan as an aggressive, militaristic state. The prospect that Japan's large stockpile of plutonium could be used to develop a nuclear weapons arsenal would pose an even more potent latent threat if that state had defences to protect its territory from China's nuclear missiles. Finally, US naval TMD systems may appear threatening to China because their mobility implies they can defend Taiwan, Japan, or other territories around the Chinese periphery.

In response to these potential threats, China may push ahead with the development of technologies that would improve the penetrability of its nuclear warheads, with the development of its own BMD systems and with the development of nuclear-armed anti-satellite systems to disrupt the infrastructure of any defences. In the past, the response to US and Russian ABM systems was to develop penetration aids for strategic missiles. China's development of multiple independently targetable re-entry vehicles (MIRVs) was delayed until recently owing to the lack of a lightweight warhead and technical hurdles associated with the post-boost vehicle. However, both options may be pursued in the future if US or Russian BMD systems are deployed. Some analysts have argued that this could precipitate an offence–defence arms race as China attempts to re-establish the effectiveness of its deterrent. US and/or Russian BMD deployments might also discourage China from engaging in future arms control agreements because it would have less incentive to limit the size of its arsenal.

The issue of missile defence deployment by the US, and possibly by Russia, is looked upon with anxiety in France, where there are concerns over the future of the ABM Treaty. Even though France's arms industry has expressed interest in anti-missile technology, the French government fears that the development of extended missile defences would undermine its nuclear deterrent. If a race in BMD technologies were to take place, France might feel pressured to stop its arms control efforts and reverse the present trend towards lower nuclear spending.

To date, the UK has also been cautious in embracing the concept of missile defence. Official statements indicate that the UK does have 'an active interest' in BMD, has been engaged with the US and France on this issue, and is involved in the NATO group which has been convened to study BMD. However, this interest does not extend to the Medium Extended Air Defence System (MEADS) being developed by some of its NATO partners. While it has been accepted that there is a need for a theatre defence capability to protect UK forces performing peace enforcement missions overseas, uncertainties remain over the cost-effectiveness of any national or regional missile defence system and the impact such a development might have on the broader strategic environment.

The issue of BMD may also be having an impact in South Asia, where reports that India may acquire, or has acquired, an advanced air defence system from Russia are said to have created a crisis of confidence in Islamabad in its own offensive capabilities. Pakistan's policymakers may fear they will now be vulnerable to a disarming first strike by India, which would then rely on its missile defences to counter any Pakistani missiles not destroyed on the ground. It is possible that these strategic vulnerabilities provoked Pakistan's decision to adopt a more aggressive nuclear strategy, based on the early use of its nuclear forces in the event of a conflict in order to penetrate India's defences.

The future development and deployment of effective missile defences could affect the perception of the utility of nuclear weapons in several countries. A country that possesses an effective defence might be persuaded to reduce its reliance on nuclear weapons, especially when the costs associated with maintaining and modernizing a nuclear stockpile are considered. However, it is also possible that countries might respond by enhancing the penetrability of their nuclear delivery systems. It is difficult to predict which outcome is more likely, and to a large extent this will be dependent on other first- and second-order shapers. Nevertheless, it is possible to postulate that in the short to medium term perceptions of the utility of nuclear weapons (even for states such as the US and Israel, which are at the cutting edge of missile technology) will not radically alter as a direct result of work on missile defence. This is because of the significant technical difficulties and huge cost associated with the development of such systems. Missile defences are more likely to be deployed in order to supplement, rather than to replace, nuclear ordnance. But they could also be deployed by NNWS, thereby opening up a new set of strategic issues. For on what basis can a NWS legitimately deny a NNWS the right to defend itself against an offensive weapon it does not itself possess, and which therefore should have no effect on the stability of existing relationships between the NWS?

Critics have argued that, in the longer term, there is a possibility of a missile technology race between the most advanced states for missiles of improved accuracy and longer range, and weapons designed to destroy or disable those missiles at various stages of their flight path. This competition between missiles and anti-missiles may take place alongside attempts to maintain existing nuclear weapons designs. Concerns over the safety of nuclear weapons may diminish incentives to maintain the hair-trigger posture of nuclear forces, leading to decisions that could undermine their deterrent effect. In short, the existence of high-tech conventional weapons and defensive missiles capable of dealing with all potential threats, including WMD attack, may mean that the states possessing these capabilities will be less willing to continue to take the risks associated with WMD and will opt for a policy of seeking to ban all such weapons.

A new generation of nuclear weapons?

Whereas developments in precision weaponry can be tested and evaluated in military exercises, anti-terrorist operations and minor wars, entry into force of the Comprehensive Test Ban Treaty would mean that this would no longer be possible with nuclear weapons. This has led to speculation over whether certain states could and would attempt to develop a new range of nuclear weapons without nuclear explosive testing. Given the quantum leap in practical knowledge required for such advances in nuclear technology, and the history of the development of testable weapons of greater military utility, this outcome does not seem likely. Policy-makers and technologists are more likely to be concerned with ways of maintaining existing nuclear weapons designs and sustaining the competence of the design teams if the CTBT enters into force, rather than with ways of developing and deploying nuclear weapons based on different scientific concepts.

Although there has been a great deal of speculation over the evolution of a new generation of low-yield nuclear weapons, the financial and political costs of developing such weapons could outweigh the benefit in deterrent and military terms. The development of pure fusion warheads would be expensive, take many years, be very uncertain technically, and require tests which would be detectable at high yields and contravene the CTBT. In addition, at low yield, a fusion weapon would not possess the explosive potential deemed necessary for deterrence, and its utility in tactical terms would be limited because such requirements are increasingly being met by other technologies.

It is also unlikely there will be a push for the development of more powerful explosive devices. Designs for deliverable warheads ranging up to 100 megatons of HE energy already exist, but only about one per cent of this explosive power has actually been deployed in stockpiled weapons. The evolution in accuracy of strike and defensive systems has led to a reduction in the yields of warheads in service to tens of kilotons. Moreover, the changing nature of warfare is likely to lead technologists to focus on the development of incendiary weapons, which differ in principle from explosive devices in that they do not deliver lethal energy but instead feed on specific targets and spread their energy to others.

Technology and attitudes to disarmament

Experimentation with fusion technology and other nuclear energy possibilities is likely to continue as states investigate their possible civil benefits. This raises difficult questions for arms control and disarmament because of the dual-use nature of some of the technology utilized in civil nuclear programmes, and because it may be argued that the experimental capabilities developed through such programmes improve the theoretical competence of weapon designers to construct the fission and fusion stages of nuclear explosive devices. Will it be possible to reassure states over the issue of a potential 'breakout' from an arms control agreement while such knowledge and expertise exist, and while dual-use possibilities remain unconstrained? And how can such constraints be constructed in the face of commercial and scientific opposition to enhanced controls and intrusive inspections? These are some of the serious hurdles that must be overcome if there is to be any chance of stabilizing global arsenals at low levels and then moving to a total ban on nuclear explosive devices.

SECOND-ORDER SHAPERS

Introduction

Although military threat perceptions and strategic relations continue to dominate nuclear policy-making, less obvious shapers of nuclear policy may in future play an increasingly significant role. These include domestic political and economic factors, changing conceptions of security, and the evolution of arms limitation regimes.

Domestic political and economic factors

Public opinion

Although it remains a difficult and controversial issue, there is evidence that public opinion can influence nuclear policy-makers. There is a striking congruence between views expressed in popular opinion polls and the nuclear policies of the states in which these polls were conducted. A national public opinion survey in the US, conducted in 1997 on behalf of the Henry L. Stimson Center, Washington, DC, provides an interesting illustration of this point. The survey revealed that although the majority of US citizens supported the long-term elimination of nuclear weapons, they believed that the US should maintain, and even improve, its nuclear capabilities. Survey respondents identified China, rather than Russia, as the state posing the most serious long-term challenge to the US, and rogue states as the most serious short-term risk. The survey therefore indicated strong parallels between the views expressed by the US public and those expressed by the Clinton administration. Polls show that there is a similar congruence between nuclear policy and public opinion in France and Israel.

A stronger case can be made for a link between public opinion and specific areas of nuclear policy. Public opposition to excessive defence spending in France, the UK and the US (expressed in opinion polls, newspaper articles, televised public discussions and qualitative studies) appears to have been taken seriously by the administrations in question. Whether public sensitivity over this issue or other factors were the key drivers towards cuts in nuclear spending is open to question, but feedback from policy-makers suggests that public opinion was an important consideration. This appears to have been the case in the UK's Strategic Defence Review, during which members of the public were encouraged to express their views in writing. The important point here is that post-Cold War governments, in the West at least, are willing to listen to public views over the nuclear issue and appear to be amenable to making concessions where possible.

This apparent responsiveness to public opinion may have a significant impact on other areas of nuclear policy in the future. At the moment public debate about nuclear weapons in the West has a lower salience than other domestic issues. However, it is possible that this could change. There could be a mass movement against nuclear weapons if public perceptions of their utility or of the credibility of nuclear deterrence were undermined by events (such as a regional nuclear war). Alternatively, there could be a movement in favour of upgrading capabilities if a new or overwhelming threat emerged. It has been argued that the nuclear policies of India and Pakistan have recently been influenced in this way. Public opinion in both states has traditionally been more concerned about the problems of poverty, economic stability, terrorism and ethnic conflict. Yet, possibly in response to changes in the strategic environment and resultant increases in threat perceptions, public attitudes in both countries have changed; the nuclear issue has sparked widespread public support for a more overt nuclear posture, and this is believed to have been an important factor in the decisions to test in May 1998 and subsequently.

Opinion formers in the NWS – such as those within the strategic and academic communities, and relevant non-governmental organizations (NGOs) – are divided over the issue of whether, and in what ways, nuclear

policy should change to meet new strategic requirements. Many, however, concur with those in policy-
making circles who consider that nuclear weapons have
retained their importance as guarantors of national
security and instruments of war prevention. What is
interesting is that in the US, the UK and France, external
expert opinion is being sought by policy-makers. In the
UK, for example, efforts to involve non-governmental
actors in the policy process have been highly publicized
in order to display a greater level of openness. This
publicity in itself is a significant development, showing
that in the post-Cold War world, some governments
want to be seen to be more responsive to broader public
suggestions where defence issues are concerned.

Political parties and democracy

The question of whether the self-interests of political
parties can influence nuclear policy is often ignored,
partly because that policy involves complex issues, and
partly because there is currently a high degree of
consensus between the major political parties in the
NWS over nuclear issues. This has not always been the
case and, moreover, may not recently have been the case
in India. India's decision to abandon years of nuclear
ambiguity cannot be fully understood unless the con-
sistent pro-nuclear views held by the Bharatiya Janata
Party (BJP) are factored into the analysis.

This example of the influence of domestic political
parties on nuclear policy leads to a set of broader questions over whether democracy promotes nuclear disarmament and nuclear restraint. It would be interesting to

32

speculate whether democracy in China or the DPRK would result in a more responsive attitude by those states to arms control and non-proliferation initiatives. In the case of India, a democratic state, the political position of the BJP led to the promotion of a more overt nuclear weapons posture. In addition, until recently the Russian Duma has demonstrated its reluctance to ratify START II, and the US Congress its opposition to the CTBT. Should these examples throw doubt on democratic peace theory? These are difficult questions to which there are no easy answers. But what the Indian case illustrates is that the domestic shapers of nuclear policy are highly complex, and cannot be generalized in the same way as those dynamics of nuclear proliferation that are largely derived from international systemic perspectives. Factors such as the type of political system operating within the state must be seen in a broader domestic context that includes strategic culture and levels of political stability, territorial integrity and social cohesion.

Economic factors

At the end of the Cold War, more attention was focused on the life-cycle costs of nuclear forces and the opportunity costs involved in developing and maintaining them. Increased awareness of costs and expectations of the 'peace dividend' have influenced the decisions of the NATO allies to dramatically reduce spending on nuclear weapons. Does this indicate that economic factors are acting as a brake on nuclear-weapon development, and that the desire to reduce defence expenditure is driving nuclear disarmament forward in the West?

Until recently, this appeared to be the case. However, the US decision to approve a budget of $10.5 billion to deploy a NMD could change these dynamics. This allocation of resources suggests that US threat perceptions are currently significantly greater than some analysts had assumed. The nuclear threat from the former Soviet Union appears to have been replaced by a number of new threats involving WMD attack by 'rogue' states, by non-state terrorist actors, or possibly by a hostile China, as well as a resurgent and antagonistic Russia. The Clinton administration's desire to cut back defence spending appears to have been outweighed by its determination to defend against these perceived threats.

Economic factors are having a prohibitive impact on maintaining Russia's nuclear arsenal. It is estimated that many of Russia's land-based ICBMs will have reached the end of their service life by 2008 and will need replacing. Similarly, Russia's nuclear-powered ballistic missile submarines (SSBNs) are gradually reaching this point and the current fleet will cease to be functional in 15–20 years. Despite this, reports indicate that, as a result of budgetary constraints, the modernization programme is proceeding more slowly than anticipated. Development of the SS-27 land-based ICBM is on schedule, but development of the SS-NX-28 submarine-launched ballistic missile (SLBM), a new SSBN and a new air-launched cruise missile (ALCM) is lagging. Even if the technical problems encountered in developing these systems are resolved, the US does not believe that Russia will have the necessary funds to deploy them. This will force Russia down to START II levels by 2005.

Economic constraints are partly responsible for Russia's force posture. Large sections of its strategic arsenal are now more vulnerable than they were during the Cold War because Russia lacks the resources to operate most of its SLBMs and mobile land-based systems in a survivable mode. They are now tied up in port or confined to their garrisons where they would be vulnerable to a pre-emptive strike. Russian command and control systems are considered to be equally open to such an attack. These concerns are compounded by US pre-emptive strike capabilities and conventionally armed precision guided munitions. Russia's ability to finance any military solutions to these vulnerabilities is restricted, and consequently its current force posture is likely to remain on hair-trigger alert unless relations with the US and China improve and residual distrust from the Cold War period disappears completely.

There are reports that financial problems may also be hindering China's defence modernization programme. There is a considerable debate over the extent of China's defence spending, with US estimates ranging from a budget of $28–45 billion to $140 billion in 1995, and official Chinese estimates putting the figure at around $8 billion. Whatever the actual figure, there are signs that China has been struggling to balance the demands of the military against the civilian budget. According to the 1995 Statement on Defence, China has placed defence spending in a position subordinate to, and in the service of, overall national economic construction. Most of the open literature on China supports this official declaration, showing that budgetary constraints are undermining China's military production and arms build-up and that this trend seems set to continue for the foreseeable future.

China's budget is constantly under pressure, with many competing needs for infrastructure development, support to state enterprises, and the administrative services of government. Despite predictions of rapid economic growth, China may not be able to meet these heavy demands. Beijing is also having difficulties developing a sufficiently high level of quality in production and technology. China's economic boom may be partly responsible for this, as skilled workers have been moving from poorly paid positions in the defence establishment into more profitable jobs in the private sector. Budgetary constraints have prevented Beijing from sufficiently increasing wages in the public sector to avert this 'brain drain'.

Together, these constraints may slow the pace of China's nuclear development and widen the gap between the nuclear ambitions that the West attributes to China and the actual progress that Beijing will be able to make in its nuclear development. The most likely consequences of this are that China will try to keep the West guessing about its nuclear capabilities by resisting pressure to increase transparency, and that it will avoid engaging in negotiations aimed at drawing it into the nuclear reductions process, especially if the US deploys its proposed NMD.

There are few signs that economic constraints have been influencing nuclear policy-making in India or Pakistan. Threat perceptions are extremely high in these states and policy-makers have been willing to accept large future economic costs in order to try to increase their security through weaponization. The nuclear tests by India and Pakistan went ahead despite the threat of international sanctions. A further indication of governmental priorities was that, in India's case, it was reported than an official government-sponsored study had concluded that Indian economic development could be set back by 10–15 years if the tests proceeded.[3]

India's defence budget increased from US $7,810 million in 1987 to US $8,333 million in 1996. Although this overall figure does not constitute a major increase, New Delhi's decision to spend 10 per cent of this budget on military research and development (R&D) is significant. It is thought that most of this expenditure is being used to bring a number of projects, such as the Integrated Guided Missile Development Plan (IGMDP), from full-scale development to production. In Pakistan's case, it has been estimated that a large proportion of the national budget is spent on defence, much of which goes to fund the nuclear and missile programmes. These levels of spending are set to remain high, and even increase, until threat perceptions reduce and the belief that prestige is associated with the possession of nuclear weapons diminishes.

Israel's government has recently been under pressure to reduce its defence budget. Since the early 1990s, Israel's economy has been slowing down, unemployment has been rising, and the national debt has been growing. However, Israeli threat perceptions remain high, and there is no evidence to suggest that spending on the nuclear weapons capability has been reduced in recent years.

[3] *Sydney Morning Herald,* 13 August 1997.

Changing conceptions of security

Second-order shapers are unlikely to replace traditional military shapers of nuclear policy unless conceptions of security are comprehensively revised and adjusted. Although there has been some movement away from the Cold War preoccupation with viewing security in specifically military terms, the statements and actions of the NWS and the *de facto* NWS show that although security is not regarded as an exclusively military concern, the military dimension continues to dominate thinking. While this situation continues, progress in arms control and disarmament may remain slow and limited.

However, the focus on the military dimension of security could diminish in response to events. Studies have noted that political instability in some regions of the world may be attributable to population stresses, group identity disputes and a lack of resources. If this trend continues and the developing world remains trapped in what has been termed the cycle of deprivation, there may be an even greater potential for instability and conflict in the period through to 2030. Moreover, some analysts have argued that in the intervening time-frame perceptions of security could be affected by environmental challenges such as climate change, water scarcity and pollution problems.

Willingness to consider deep cuts in nuclear weapons arsenals and to strive for a NWFW may be greater in a context of economic and environmental catastrophes. Nuclear weapons might have little utility in a situation of uncontrolled population growth, mass migration and resource scarcity. If such threats did begin to escalate, there might be a shift in thinking away from the narrower requirements of national security to the broader problem of how to deal with these global economic and environmental threats.

Writers on the effects of globalization have suggested that shifts in thinking about security could be reinforced if the power of international financial institutions eroded further the viability of the state and its claims to sovereignty over a defined territory. One outcome of such a development could be a growing economic, technological and political interconnectedness, which would restrict any one state's capacity to act. It has been argued that in such a world, nuclear weapons would have a dramatically reduced relevance.

On the other hand, in the shorter term, the uneven effects of globalization and development may lead to greater instability in some regions by generating incentives for poorer states to acquire WMD for use as bargaining chips against richer states. This could lead to the emergence of what has been termed a 'zone of instability', giving the states of the developed world justification for the retention of their own nuclear arsenals to deter the aggressive actions of others. NATO's new Strategic Concept shows some indication that the more holistic approach to security which emerged in the West at the end of the Cold War may have been halted in response to the threat of WMD attack by states wishing to challenge the status quo. This is not to say that worst-case scenario thinking will now dominate NATO's approach to security, as the Alliance has promised to examine possibilities for further disarmament initiatives.

It does, however, indicate that in a world of regional instability and uneven economic development, traditional conceptions of security will change only slowly, despite the emergence of new, non-military security challenges.

The evolution of arms management and limitation regimes

The period since the Second World War has seen major advances in the development of arms control arrangements. While early arms control treaties relied on simple statements of agreement, a gradual development has taken place both in the number of components in an agreement and in the comprehensiveness of its drafting. The 'diplomatic technology' for arms control is now very highly developed, covering internal legal requirements of treaty membership, implicit or explicit export controls, security assurances and guarantees, verification measures and administrative processes. However, despite intensive diplomatic activity and progress 'on paper', the effectiveness of arms control measures has been limited by serious obstacles, both general and treaty-specific. Until these obstacles can be overcome, perceptions of military threat will continue to dominate nuclear policy-making, thus limiting the prospects for movement towards a NWFW.

It is possible to identify three major obstacles to arms control initiatives in the current environment. First, there is the non-state problem. The idea of enhanced security through state-to-state agreements on arms control is losing ground to concerns about terrorism, against which treaties are largely ineffective. The loss of control of fissile materials in the former Soviet Union, and claims concerning the relative ease of production of devastating biological weapons, have exacerbated this problem. It is undermining the confidence of governments in arms control agreements and could lead to the erosion of support for the traditional arms control approach among the public and in state legislatures.

The second problem is the growing view that arms control treaties, which may require years of negotiation, use valuable legislative time for ratification and create large and expensive bureaucracies, are only adhered to by states which would have behaved in this manner in any case, and are easily set aside when circumstances change. The alternative is seen to be the use of economic and, if necessary, military coercion to force states to desist from seeking what are viewed as inappropriate weapon systems.

The third problem, which is affecting both the maintenance and the development of arms control regimes, is the conflict between the need to ensure effective export control over dual-use items and the demand of developing countries for free access to advanced technology.

A number of problems with specific treaties are also hampering progress in arms control. For example, the effectiveness of the Nuclear Non-Proliferation Treaty (NPT) is currently undermined by tensions arising from resentment of the status of the NWS, regional conflicts and development agendas. Major new accessions will depend on peaceful resolution of the Arab–Israeli and India–Pakistan disputes, and on the willingness of the NWS to demonstrate their commitment to nuclear

41

disarmament. Since the agreement to extend the NPT indefinitely in 1995, there has been little progress in either regard.

The US–Russia bilateral nuclear arms reduction process is already suffering from problems of decommissioning to previously agreed levels. Talk of transforming START from a bilateral to a multilateral process may also meet with resistance. China, France and the UK might not wish to be drawn into the reduction process as they believe they already have a minimum credible deterrent force. Moreover, it is possible that a future US administration could support the non-inclusion of these states to avoid setting standards for minimum deterrence, which could generate demands for the United States to reduce to similar nuclear force levels.

The threat posed by biological weapons and the difficulty of maintaining an international control regime to check the proliferation of offensive biological warfare capabilities are also major obstacles to progress in nuclear arms control. Confidence in the effectiveness of the Bacteriological and Toxins Weapons Convention (BTWC) to limit such capabilities is diminished by the belief that it is difficult to prove that a state is actively engaged in an offensive, and therefore illegal, biological weapons programme. Agreement on a Verification Protocol to this Convention may do little to change these perceptions. The insecurity generated by this situation is further exacerbated by the knowledge that modern fermentation procedures allow for rapid and inexpensive production of biological agents, and that to go from laboratory quantities to weapons quantities of these agents takes a matter of days or weeks, rather than years. This has had the effect of reinforcing the commitment of the NWS to their nuclear deterrent capabilities. Moreover, it has fuelled the US debate over the advantages of developing a NMD and increased the possibility that existing arms control treaties, such as the ABM Treaty, could be revised or abandoned in the light of strategic contingencies.

The obstacles to the conclusion of new arms control agreements and the problems associated with existing treaties might lead to the mistaken assumption that these measures have only a small role to play in promoting nuclear disarmament and non-proliferation. It is fair to say that, unless the international political environment and conceptions of security undergo major changes, the effectiveness of such agreements will always be in some doubt. However, an important effect of arms control to date has been the creation of norms against the use or the development of certain weapons systems, and in favour of disarmament. The emergence of the New Agenda Coalition (NAC) shows that there is growing international support for nuclear non-proliferation and disarmament, even though current political conditions are preventing significant progress towards these goals.

A further role of arms control agreements is that they can contribute to confidence-building, even if their effects are limited. Transparency measures are particularly important in this regard, as they can reduce threat perceptions and build greater trust between adversaries. The idea that transparency enhances security policy therefore needs to be strengthened. Arms control has provided for this not only through verification provisions in formal treaties, but also through specific confidence-building measures and procedures, such as the UN conventional arms register.

Despite the hurdles, there have been some significant successes in implementing disarmament and non-proliferation agreements since the end of the Cold War, especially at the regional level. At present 107 states are parties to Nuclear-Weapon-Free Zones (NWFZs), which cover 50 per cent of the world's landmass. The Latin American, South Pacific, Southeast Asian and African NWFZs have banned nuclear weapons within their specified territory, tasked the International Atomic Energy Agency (IAEA) with verification responsibilities and established permanent treaty organs. In doing so, such agreements play a vital role in confidence-building among neighbouring states in many parts of the world. The Southeast Asian and African treaties, in particular, have set more far-reaching non-proliferation and disarmament goals than the global regimes. Both contain compliance provisions and, in addition, the Pelindaba Treaty contains measures for the destruction of existing devices, commitments on conditions for exports to NNWS, physical protection requirements, and prohibition of attacks on peaceful nuclear installations in the African NWFZ. Although members of potential NWFZs are prone to disagreements over the boundaries of such zones, and although such treaties do not constitute substitutes for effective global regimes, they do help to bring the prospect of a NWFW closer by contributing to the evolution of the non-proliferation and non-stationing norms.

It has been argued that the CTBT is significant more for its environmental impact than for its function as an arms control and non-proliferation measure. Many believe that even if the Treaty does enter into force – and this is still dependent on ratification by the 44 states specified in the preamble as the key ones for the purposes of the Treaty, and (above all) on ratification by the US – the removal of the option to conduct nuclear tests will not necessarily stem vertical or horizontal nuclear proliferation. Technologically advanced states will be able to simulate tests if they wish to do so. Moreover, the experiences of Israel and South Africa suggest that states need not openly demonstrate a nuclear capability in order to develop nuclear weapons or a deterrent: opaque deterrence can suffice. However, others have argued that the CTBT will have a significant impact by placing crucial restrictions on further technological progress. The reluctance of the US, China, India, Pakistan, Israel and the DPRK to ratify the Treaty adds credibility to these claims.

Finally, depending on its components, a Fissile Material Cut-off Treaty (FMCT) could constitute a major step towards disarmament. At the moment negotiations over this Treaty are being hampered by the positions held both by the NWS and by some of the NNWS. Calls to place all pre-existing stocks of fissile materials under safeguards are being resisted (and are likely to continue to be resisted) by the NWS, which argue that only future stocks should be included in a FMCT. It may be possible to reach a compromise over this issue, if the NWS agree to place surplus, rather than all, fissile materials in military stockpiles under the supervision of the IAEA.

However, this solution could be complicated by disagreements over what constitutes excess materials. It would also leave open the issue of how to persuade India, Israel and Pakistan to accept the limitations a FMCT would impose upon them. Yet if a compromise is reached, the FMCT is likely to constitute a major step in dealing with the dangers posed by fissile materials, as well as one of the basic building blocks for a fissile-material-led disarmament process.

THIRD-ORDER SHAPERS

Introduction

Third-order shapers are those activities that are considered vital to future nuclear limitation processes, including disarmament strategies, verification techniques and issues of compliance. Such activities are classed as third-order shapers because they are unlikely to function as the primary factors influencing nuclear policy until nuclear weapons are perceived by key policy-makers to have a reduced military or political utility. If such a change does occur, third-order shapers are likely to influence the nuclear future or futures that emerge. In the meantime, they will have an important role to play in the debate over whether a move to zero is desirable or feasible and how it could be achieved. Moreover, developments in verification techniques and compliance will be among the many factors influencing the threat perceptions and security interests of the NWS and the *de facto* NWS.

At present, these areas are under-researched and any discussion of them raises more questions than it answers.

That said, the process of identifying the crucial questions is an important exercise in itself. Two issues are particularly relevant in this respect. First, what constitutes a world of zero nuclear weapons? Second, how might zero be achieved? Answers to this question are obviously dependent on what is specifically meant by zero, but some general ideas are discussed in the next section.

What would constitute a world free of nuclear weapons?

Although nuclear disarmament has been a potent political goal for over half a century, in that period little detailed analysis has been undertaken to determine precisely what a world without nuclear weapons would involve. Once a nuclear device had been exploded and the use of nuclear weapons demonstrated, it was difficult to see how the ability to construct nuclear weapons could be eliminated. It meant that control over this technology was deemed to be possible only by preventing the acquisition of the fissile materials needed to manufacture nuclear explosive devices. Hence, the central element in the Baruch Plan of 1946, the IAEA safeguards system and the NPT was the denial of fissile materials to potential national nuclear weapon programmes. Thus, one perspective of a NWFW is that it would involve putting all fissile material under a system of international supervision, with the disarmament process itself being 'fissile-material-led', whereby an increasing percentage of the global total of this material would be placed under such supervision. Others argue that these arrangements will necessarily be weak if fissile material is constantly being produced in nuclear reactors and

47

uranium enrichment plants, and that a truly effective NWFW can be achieved only by closing them down and disposing of existing fissile materials in a manner which prevents their retrieval.

Another view of a NWFW is that it should rest on a political commitment not to acquire nuclear weapons. Thus, a crucial element would be the negotiation of a Nuclear Weapons Convention embodying such a commitment. This, however, begs the question of whether the commitment would solely involve dismantling nuclear weapons or would also cover the capability to manufacture and maintain them. If the first option is chosen, would the objective be to dismantle and ultimately destroy all the components together with those comprising their delivery systems, or would a more simple separation of the ordnance from the delivery system be preferred? If manufacturing and maintenance capabilities were to be destroyed, would this process encompass the dismantling of all the components in the weapons and the delivery system, as well as the infrastructure involved in their manufacture? Finally, would all detailed knowledge and experience of the manufacture of both ordnance and delivery systems need to be eliminated, and would bans be required on certain of the key dual-use technologies?

What is apparent from the above is that there are likely to exist several technical variations in what is understood to be a NWFW. While some attention has been paid to this issue, there still appears to be a need for more detailed studies of what zero means in the context of a nuclear disarmament process and how such a goal might be pursued in practice.

Disarmament strategies

Until a consensus is reached over how a NWFW could be achieved, none of the NWS is likely to take steps to move below a minimum nuclear deterrent. At least three alternative strategies can be envisaged to enable a move to zero to occur:

- the time-bound framework/blueprint approach;
- the incremental/adaptive approach;
- the *de facto* disarmament/virtual nuclear arsenals (VNAs)/indirect approach.

In addition, zero might be achieved by default, if nuclear weapons are not replaced for economic or political reasons, or are superseded by the use of non-nuclear technologies. However, it is difficult to describe this as a strategy.

The time-bound framework/blueprint approach

Proponents of this strategy argue that if nuclear systems have been constructed within a given time-frame, there is no reason why they cannot be dismantled in a similar way. Political will should enable the necessary resources to be committed to this objective. The key issue in moving to zero is therefore to mobilize domestic and international support for a political agreement which would commit states to such a process. Critics of this approach argue that political agreement will only be forthcoming if the security threats, methods of thinking and perceptions which led to nuclear arming can be removed or changed, and an environment supportive of moving to zero created.

The incremental/adaptive approach

Those who argue for this approach believe that zero will only be reached if a sequential series of events occurs, in which actions and negotiated agreements change perceptions, which in turn would enable further developments to occur or agreements to be negotiated: in short, a confidence-building process needs to be created and sustained. Thus, what is seen as necessary is to pursue many of the steps advocated in the first strategy, but without the overall framework of time. This was the approach taken by the Principles and Objectives document agreed by the 1995 NPT Review and Extension Conference, and appears to be the basis of the proposals advocated by the eight states involved in the NAC that have had a major impact on the proceedings of the First Committee of the UN General Assembly since 1998.

The de facto disarmament/VNAs/indirect approach

This approach arises from the ideas of those seeking to lessen the risks of inadvertent use of nuclear forces by removing them from hair-trigger deployment arrangements. It involves de-targeting and de-mounting warheads from missiles or removing guidance systems from them, thus ensuring that they would take longer to respond to an order to fire. One consequence of pursuing such changes in operating procedures is that warheads might eventually be removed to central stores, which could then be placed under international supervision. Although states would retain notional custody of their nuclear warheads, they would become a reserve capability, which over time could become less relevant to the state's security policy. This approach would be supported by moves to place increasing percentages of the fissile materials in NWS under IAEA safeguards. The logical consequence of both strands of policy would be a slow movement to a *de facto* state of zero nuclear weapons, though a major stumbling block identified in this process has been the question of how to deal with SLBMs. It is also argued that it might encourage dangerous reconstitution races along 1914 lines and a high risk of first strikes, if the time-scale for reconstitution were very short.

Verification techniques and frameworks

Whichever strategy is decided upon, the NWS will only continue with, and *de facto* NWS will only engage in, nuclear disarmament when they believe this to be in their political and security interests. The evolution of a strong verification system will therefore be vital, as the effectiveness of verification measures will be a key yardstick by which states will measure their security interests. Moreover, the importance of this issue is likely to increase exponentially if the world moves further towards lower numbers and eventually towards a zero option, as the relative benefits to states that cheat, and the costs to compliant states, increase.

Two deceptively simple questions lie at the heart of the verification debate. First, what needs to be verified to demonstrate compliance? Second, what mechanisms are needed to ensure that obligations are being fulfilled?

What needs to be verified?

Verification requirements are likely to change as numbers decrease. Within a disarmed world, there may be a need for a comprehensive system of verification for nuclear disarmament focusing on several technologies. Until that stage is reached, nuclear warheads, delivery systems and fissile materials are likely to be the principal concerns of any verification system.

Warheads For disarmament to move forward, a framework will have to be created to verify ceilings on warheads and to address non-compliance issues that may arise. This would imply an agreement containing some or all of the following elements:

- definitions of what is being limited (for example, active warheads only, active and reserve warheads, or active and reserve warheads and those that have been retired but have yet to go through a dismantling plant);

- a process for declaring stocks of warheads in the agreed categories, and the quantities of fissile materials within them;

- a process for verifying the accuracy of the initial declarations of the stocks of warheads and the quantities of fissile materials contained within them, and for resolving any discrepancies;

- a process for declaring national nuclear weapon dismantling and manufacturing facilities, and for monitoring all warheads entering and leaving such facilities in order to verify any differences in the quantities of fissile material between them; and

- a process for constraining the ability of a state rapidly to break away from the agreement and reconstitute a large arsenal (for example, by constraints on nuclear and non-nuclear components and by limiting the number of warheads on each delivery system).

These tasks suggest a need to develop methods to ensure that no changes have been made to a warhead, and methods to track or ban certain non-warhead configurations of non-nuclear components and/or fissile materials. Work is also needed to design techniques for rapidly, safely and cheaply rendering weapon-pits unsuitable for re-use; for conducting non-intrusive measurements of the quantities and composition of fissile materials in warheads; and for non-intrusive monitoring of weapon dismantling and construction plants and operational deployment sites. Monitoring arrangements will also be required for de-alerting measures at warhead storage sites, such as the removal of warheads from delivery systems.

Delivery systems If nuclear disarmament is to continue, a framework will be required to verify ceilings on delivery vehicles and to address non-compliance issues. One problem that will arise immediately is the dual-use nature of many of these systems, either as delivery systems for conventional ordnance or, in the case of ballistic missiles, as potential satellite launchers. Such a framework would need to specify which missiles, cruise missiles or aircraft are being numerically limited, in the light of these dual-use issues. It would also require the development of at least three types of verification processes. First, a process for declaring the numbers of operational and reserve delivery systems, and the development of techniques for uniquely identifying those to be included within a ceiling. Second, a process for declaring the numbers and identities of warheads to be carried on each type of delivery system or carrier vehicle (such as submarine or aircraft) and for verifying that these numbers have not been exceeded. Third, a process for verifying the dismantling/destruction/conversion to other use of specified delivery systems and of their replacement with new delivery systems.

These tasks suggest a need for technical work to distinguish treaty-limited delivery systems from others and to identify each individual delivery system for accounting purposes. It would also require work on techniques to ensure the non-intrusive measurement of the number of warheads on any one delivery system or carrier vehicle, and their identification, and to monitor inputs/outputs from declared delivery system/carrier vehicle production and destruction plants.

Fissile materials Any state wishing to build a clandestine nuclear arsenal needs access to fissile materials. Stockpiles of fissile materials therefore need to be monitored and agreements reached on discontinuing the production of weapons-grade fissile materials and on the disposal of surplus stocks. Declarations of all fissile materials within the jurisdiction of a state should be made to the IAEA or a fissile material agency created specifically for this purpose. Verification of these declarations by that agency would be required to cover a range of locations for these fissile materials, including supplies in warheads; buffer stocks of materials for warhead re-manufacture and submarine fuel manufacture; stocks in submarine fuel fabrication plants; fabricated submarine fuel and other military reactor fuel; irradiated submarine fuel in storage ponds; and declared former military stocks.

Such an arrangement would almost certainly utilize techniques already being implemented by the IAEA to enhance the NPT safeguards system, as well as those being discussed in the IAEA–Russian–US trilateral negotiations on verification of surplus plutonium stocks. More specifically, it would involve developing a list of materials to be monitored; accountancy and monitoring techniques for verifying fissile materials in warheads, submarine fuel and weapon facility buffer stocks; techniques for remote detection of clandestine enrichment and reprocessing plants, and weapon production facilities; and enhanced techniques for remote monitoring of declared enrichment and reprocessing plants and storage facilities.

How will verification take place?

Tagging or bar-coding The effect of implementing the above frameworks fully would be to allow for the monitoring of all fissile materials within a state, all nuclear warheads and their delivery systems, and the process of dismantling and re-manufacturing such warheads when decisions are made to sustain the safety and reliability of a national stockpile. This monitoring and accounting system might be assisted by the assignment of a unique identity tag or bar-code to each warhead or delivery system. Such tags, which would need to be impossible to destroy or reproduce, could be used to monitor the existence of specific warheads and delivery systems regularly in a non-intrusive manner, and to confirm the identity of these artefacts when they are moved into a facility to be re-manufactured or dismantled and destroyed.

Centralized and decentralized verification Just as important as the technologies and techniques of verification will be the structures set up to operate those procedures. Existing international agreements can be divided into two types, with different basic structures for organizing verification and compliance monitoring: centralized, with a body established for the task; and decentralized, where the process is carried out at a state-to-state level. Examples of centralized verification include the work of the Organization for the Prohibition of Chemical Weapons (OPCW) in verifying the Chemical Weapons Convention (CWC) and that of the IAEA in operating safeguards in support of the NPT. Examples of agreements with decentralized verification include most bilateral treaties, such as the START Treaties, and the multilateral Conventional Armed Forces in Europe (CFE) Treaty. A key decision for the participants in a regime for nuclear weapons limitation and disarmament will be whether to adopt centralized or decentralized verification, or some mixture of the two that may utilize the advantages of each. This optimum arrangement may change as the process of nuclear disarmament continues.

For example, while the next round of nuclear arms control negotiations will be limited to the US and Russia, at some stage other states may become involved in the talks. The first round of these may be a treaty to put a cap on all types of nuclear weapons held by all of the NWS, a Nuclear Arms Reduction Treaty (NART). Verification for this may have characteristics closer to confidence-building and transparency measures than to stringent verification. Within this, each state would be responsible for its own verification activities. The next stage may require the NWS to move down to zero. This then brings in other issues such as the actions of the three *de facto* NWS and potentially non-compliant NPT parties. No NWS is likely to want to give up its nuclear weapon capability while the *de facto* NWS retain theirs. Nor will the NWS wish to disarm unless there is increased confidence in full compliance among the NPT states. This situation will require an interface between the decentralized verification system used by the NWS and the centralized IAEA system of safeguards covering the NPT NNWS. There may also be parallel arrangements covering the *de facto* NWS. In addition, such agreements will have to be supported by domestic legislation.

Serious obstacles Complicating the issue of how to link centralized and decentralized forms of verification is the question of how to deal with non-state actors which the verification system will not be able to control or which it may not even know about. Cooperation between those charged with internal verification and control and those tasked with implementing international activities would be required to remedy this situation, in addition to domestic legislation. However, this solution may not be applicable to states in which both the domestic legislative process and internal control are breaking down.

Verification is likely to become more difficult and more important in a world of low numbers, and still more crucial in a NWFW. The zero option for nuclear weapons will always be subject of reservations, because of the threat of breakout and the uncertain nature of the type of knowledge and capabilities required to make simple nuclear devices. Unless a verification technology or technique is developed that can successfully detect breaches in the disarmament obligations of any state, the possibility of breakout may prevent the zero option from being credible in the eyes of many policy-makers.

Issues of compliance and non-compliance

Compliance and enforcement of WMD disarmament and non-proliferation obligations have become key issues for international security, and are likely to become even more significant in the future. To a great extent, they are likely to influence the direction in which the world moves, whether it is to a high-salience, lower-salience or disarmed nuclear future. This is because non-compliant behaviour and the effectiveness of mechanisms for dealing with it have a direct impact on the threat perceptions of all states. If the procedures set up to deter, punish and reverse deviant activities fail, confidence in existing and future arms control and disarmament agreements is likely to be undermined, threatening their survival.

It is therefore crucial that discussion of the complex and controversial subject of compliance is placed high on the agendas of all states wishing to prevent a return to an anarchic high-salience nuclear world. Four core questions require particular attention:

- How should compliance with WMD obligations be demonstrated?

- What constitutes non-compliance?

- Can non-compliance be deterred?

- How should the international community respond to non-compliance?

Verifying compliance

Concerns exist that key technologies have already been disseminated and several states could be in a position to manufacture WMD in the future. Unless compliance with WMD obligations can be demonstrated, the confidence required for progress in arms control and disarmament will be lacking. Membership of the WMD regimes is the most obvious method of doing this. This, however, raises difficult questions concerning the effectiveness of their existing verification arrangements.

What constitutes non-compliance?

Effective measures to prevent non-compliant behaviour cannot be devised until there is some agreement over what constitutes non-compliance. In simple terms, any state that does not abide by its international obligations is guilty of non-compliance. The language of all treaties and agreements must therefore include a clear statement on compliance and the relevant procedures for demonstrating it. In addition, the UN Security Council President's statement of 1992 on non-proliferation requires further development. This indicated that the proliferation of

WMD is regarded as a threat to international peace and security under Chapter VII of the UN Charter, but did not suggest an appropriate response to this threat.

Because of the problems of verification and different interpretations of treaty commitments, there are likely to be very few clear-cut cases of non-compliance. However, it would be helpful to identify possible types of non-compliant behaviour and the potential risk of each situation arising. For example, analysts of non-compliance have suggested that the characteristics of the guilty party are likely to determine non-compliant activities. A technologically advanced state might pursue a high-technology route to get around its treaty obligations. A less advanced state might be more likely to violate its treaty obligations by storing WMD in secret locations – what has been called the 'bombs in the basement' scenario. These activities are likely to present different challenges to verification systems and to require different responses.

The likelihood of alternative non-compliant scenarios arising will depend on global and regional strategic, political and economic factors and on the domestic environments of the states involved. It will also be affected by the type of non-compliant behaviour involved. For example, it has been noted by Serge Sur[4] that violations relating to procedural lapses or negligence may differ in kind from those that are the product of a deliberate attempt to circumvent treaty obligations.

---

[4] Serge Sur, *Disarmament and Arms Limitation Obligations: Problems of Compliance and Enforcement*, Aldershot, Hants, Dartmouth for UNIDIR, 1994, p. 8.

Making distinctions between the types of non-compliant behaviour may therefore be important in determining the amount of effort allocated to responding to these activities.

Deterring non-compliant behaviour

The question of how non-compliant behaviour can or should be prevented is a controversial one. In 1961 Fred C. Iklé wrote that

> A potential violator will not be deterred simply by the risk that his action may be discovered. What will deter him will be the fear that what he gains from the violation will be outweighed by the loss he may suffer from the victim's reaction to it.[5]

Although Iklé's cost–benefit analysis may be questionable because it assumes both that actors are rational and that costs and benefits are known to the parties involved, it is still worth considering what types of costs would deter a potential violator. Iklé identified four such sets: the weight of world opinion; the political reaction of injured parties; the consequences of military measures taken by other states to restore the *status quo ante*; and their punitive measures to inflict political and/or military damage on the potential violator.

The question of how effective these potential costs are likely to be today in deterring non-compliant actions in different situations is not self-evident. It will depend to a great extent on the internal characteristics of the non-

---

[5] Fred C. Iklé, 'After Detection, What?', *Foreign Affairs*, Vol. 39, Fall 1961, p. 208.

compliant state, and in particular on the psychological profile of its political leader. Unless consideration is given to these factors, misperceptions could lead to serious misjudgments and mistakes, such as over-reliance on political solutions when a situation may only be open to handling by a military response and vice versa.

Responses to non-compliance

If cases of non-compliance are not responded to appropriately, WMD prohibitions could be undermined. The international community has therefore to find methods which raise the costs of non-compliant activities. As Eric Arnett[6] and others have noted, two approaches exist within the relevant literature for dealing with non-compliance once it has been detected: cooperative measures relying on the use of mediation and arbitration; and confrontational or coercive measures based on authoritative multilateral or unilateral action involving either unilateral or multilateral sanctions and the use of force. One question is how effective these different approaches can be individually, and whether they can be successfully combined.

Enforcement of non-compliance is usually viewed as a sliding scale of responses from a warning to the imposition of small penalties, to more stringent sanctions and ultimately the use of force. There are a number of problems with this approach. First, it assumes a linear chain of reactions that occur within a relatively short space of time: the detection of a breach; a decision to

[6] Eric Arnett, 'The Primacy of Politics: Cooperative versus Confrontational Approaches to Compliance', in James Brown, ed., *New Horizons and New Strategies in Arms Control*, Albuquerque, N. Mex., Sandia National Laboratories, 1998, pp. 331–52.

respond to that breach; and the implementation of a plan of action that is deemed appropriate. In reality, the process of detecting and responding to non-compliance is likely to be far more complex, as it may occur in a politically charged context possibly involving continuous decision-making over a long period of time. Under these conditions, clear-cut decisions are unlikely, and delays will work in favour of the violator. Second, the question of legitimacy is likely to compound these problems. Unless there is a clear delineation of authority on compliance, questions over whether or not the use of force is legitimate may reinforce rather than diminish WMD proliferation dynamics. To solve this problem, an international body would be required to act as the ultimate arbiter in any dispute, and its authority would need to be supported by domestic legislation.

Although the effectiveness of sanctions and of force is difficult to evaluate and their implementation complex, it is nevertheless important that states are made aware that these options will not be ruled out in cases of clear violation. In most cases of non-compliance, however, one argument often made is that a cooperative approach is probably more appropriate in the longer term than a confrontational one. But there are also problems with the consensual approach. First, although treaty conferences allow for compliance issues to be addressed, it may be difficult to use these structures for settling clear breaches of treaty obligations. Separate arbitration mechanisms need to be put in place to deal with the urgent grievances of the parties to the treaties and agreements, and with non-parties and non-state actors in clear violation of international norms. Second, it may

63

be difficult to establish negotiating mechanisms for dealing with non-compliance unless they are contained in treaties based on reciprocity. Until this happens, the privileged states are likely to be accused of using their position to impose their 'norms' upon others through the mediation process. Third, some states may use the arbitration mechanisms to obtain political leverage to achieve concessions. Some situations may merit a system of incentives to ensure compliance and build confidence, but the international community must be aware of the threat of copycat behaviour. This is likely to be a particular problem with states that remain outside existing WMD treaties and have little to lose from engaging in political blackmail.

It has been suggested that the most appropriate system of compliance would probably seek to integrate cooperative and confrontational approaches. For this dual approach to succeed, the relationship between the regulatory or monitoring mechanism, the mediation mechanism and the enforcement mechanism will have to be carefully elucidated. In several existing agreements of this kind, there has been a tendency to separate the regulatory or monitoring role from the mediation and enforcement roles, with the first entrusted to one body and the last two to another, usually the UN. The question thus raised is whether this is the most appropriate division of labour for multilateral arms control agreements or whether all the roles should be incorporated within one body.

CONCLUSIONS

This analysis of the shapers of nuclear policy has indicated that if first-order shapers retain their dominant position as the main considerations that influence nuclear policy, progress towards a nuclear disarmed world is unlikely. By contrast, it also suggests that advances in arms control, heightened awareness of the costs and limited benefits of a new nuclear arms race, and new conceptions of security could produce greater willingness to promote nuclear non-proliferation and disarmament strategies. These second-order shapers could help create the momentum towards even lower-salience nuclear futures and ultimately a NWFW, in particular if progress occurred in the development of verification and compliance procedures and a consensus was reached on how a disarmed world could be achieved and what it might involve.

However, the most likely short-to-medium term development is the emergence of regional zones where different shapers dominate. It is already apparent that globalization is not leading every region down the same path. Technological advances in conventional weaponry and BMD are reducing the salience of nuclear weapons in the West, leading to further attempts to reduce numbers. Elsewhere, the perceived utility of nuclear weapons to compensate for relative weaknesses in conventional capabilities, is increasing. This in turn is leading to the prospect of further horizontal nuclear proliferation. Thus, an international environment characterized by regional and/or asymmetrical deterrence situations is emerging. This raises questions over the security implications of such discontinuities. Will traditional conceptions of deterrence continue to function under these conditions? Will it prove more difficult to hold the line created by global nuclear arms limitation and management agreements in a world characterized by regional and/or asymmetrical deterrence relationships? If the line should break, what would be the effect of such discontinuities and asymmetries on international relations? An understanding of these issues will be vital in any attempt to postulate what the future might hold.

PART II

THREE ALTERNATIVE NUCLEAR FUTURES

Introduction

This part focuses on three 'ideal types' of nuclear future that could emerge over the next 20–30 years and beyond: a high-salience nuclear world, a lower-salience nuclear world (including a world of VNAs) and a NWFW.[7] What would be the characteristics of these different nuclear futures? What pressures could determine which nuclear future develops? What kinds of constraints might prevent the evolution of a particular nuclear future?

Three questions of terminology require clarification at this point. First, it is worth emphasizing that the nuclear futures under discussion should not be regarded as 'end-states'. This is because the term implies a state of permanence, which is highly unlikely where nuclear dynamics are concerned owing to the continued existence of the knowledge required to develop nuclear weapons – knowledge that is extremely difficult, if not impossible, to destroy. It could be prone to change, cheating and breakout, which would require a series of measures to deter and deal with such activities. These measures may need to be adjusted according to political, military and technological developments, ensuring that

[7] For some earlier thought see Sir Michael Quinlan, 'The Future of Nuclear Weapons: Policy for Western Possessors', *International Affairs*, Vol. 69, No. 3, 1993, pp. 486–88; and Michael J. Mazarr, 'Virtual Nuclear Arsenals', *Survival*, Vol. 37, 1995, pp. 7–26.

the nuclear issue will remain alive and consequently demand new policy solutions.

Second, the term 'nuclear salience' is here broadly defined to include numbers of weapons, nuclear doctrines and issues of nuclear legitimacy. High nuclear salience refers to a situation where nuclear weapons occupy a prominent position in international relations and in strategic doctrine. By contrast, low nuclear salience describes a situation where nuclear weapons assume a reduced profile in this context, while a NWFW is one in which nuclear weapons are no longer seen to have any significant political or military role in international relations, and in which zero is reached and maintained. But the world is not as simple as this categorization would suggest. The nature of the international environment is such that different levels of nuclear salience can coexist in different parts of the world. As with shapers, salience is contextual – it varies according to regional dynamics. This complicates the situation considerably. As a consequence, it is helpful to start with a discussion of salience in generic terms before addressing the question of how different regional nuclear futures could develop and the problems this poses for arms control and disarmament initiatives.

Third, in this section the shapers of nuclear policy are divided into 'pressures' and 'constraints'. The former includes the first-, second- and third-order shapers that are most likely to encourage the emergence of the particular nuclear future under discussion. The latter refers to the first-, second- and third-order shapers that are most likely to discourage such a future.

A: A high-salience nuclear future

Characteristics

A high-salience nuclear world would be one in which nuclear weapons re-emerge as the dominant factor in international relations. It would see a new spate of arms racing among the NWS, and the spread of WMD and delivery capabilities to states wishing to challenge the political-military status quo. Arms control and non-proliferation treaties would erode, resulting in greater access to fissile material, missile technology and biological and chemical weapons. Nuclear testing might be resumed by the *de facto* NWS, and begin in other states. Testing might also be resumed in the NWS. This high-salience nuclear world could be highly fragmented and be characterized by regional, as well as global, nuclear arms racing. The technologically advanced states would be driven to deploy defences against the more limited capabilities of smaller nuclear-weapon states, generating an offence–defence nuclear arms race in which numbers of both defensive systems and offensive warheads multiplied.

The uneven development of global and regional capabilities would have severe consequences for the maintenance of international and national security. In such a world, the risk of use of nuclear ordnance might be greater than during the Cold War. This is because between 1945 and1989 a very small number of states were able to exercise a high degree of centralized control over their nuclear arsenals, which had been designed to meet the technical standards of guaranteeing unacceptable retaliatory damage in the event of attack. A high-salience nuclear future might also be characterized by a mix of high and low technology in nuclear postures.

Pressures

A high-salience nuclear future is most likely to emerge as a result of adverse political and economic developments at global and regional levels. The most likely shaper would be the continued deterioration of political relations between the NWS, in particular between China, Russia and the US. This could occur as a result of further disagreements between the US and Russia over the role of NATO, the expansion of NATO or large-scale US deployment of BMD. These developments could encourage Russia to rely even more heavily on nuclear ordnance to offset its conventional military deficiencies. This, in turn, might spark a drive for more sophisticated nuclear technologies in the US, resulting in a new offence–defence arms race between the previous Cold War rivals.

A high-salience nuclear world might also follow clashes between the US and China over Taiwan, or the emergence of an expansionist government in Beijing. Given that China may currently be contemplating a substantial expansion of its own nuclear force (possibly making it the world's second-largest nuclear state by 2015), there is potential for a new nuclear arms race between the US and China should bilateral relations deteriorate.

Changes in the relationship between the US and its traditional strategic partners might also trigger regional arms racing dynamics in the Middle East and Northeast Asia. For example, the deterioration of relations between the US and Israel, or the removal of US nuclear guarantees from Japan, the Republic of Korea (ROK) or Taiwan, would greatly increase proliferation pressures in those countries. This could lead to a period where high- and low-salience regions coexist in parallel, which might eventually give rise to high salience for nuclear weapons globally.

Technological developments could also act as an important swing factor towards a high-salience nuclear future. For example, the development and deployment of US BMD might make US regional intervention more likely as a consequence of the strengthening of regional alliances and reduced risks. To the extent that the US would be more willing to intervene in regional conflicts because it would have defences to protect its forces and allies, regional states would have a greater incentive to acquire WMD to deter US intervention, although if BMD systems were effective they would choose delivery means other than ballistic missiles. This is one of the fundamental tensions prompted by BMD developments, which could undermine the intended security benefits of the system.

Another uncertainty is the longer-term effects of BMD deployments on the future strategic environment. If these were to prompt an action–reaction process between offensive and defensive missile systems, there is concern that it might provoke the collapse of existing arms control and non-proliferation treaties.

Economic factors might also play an important role. Any collapse of the global economic system could lead states to refuse to engage in political and economic cooperation. Instead, governments would revert to policies based on economic protectionism and, if the past is any guide, extreme forms of national military self-assertion might emerge. Under these conditions, the acquisition of nuclear ordnance and delivery capabilities might be assisted by the collapse of one or more of the NWS and/ or the disintegration of arms control treaties, leading to the rapid proliferation of WMD among states seeking military protection and political and economic bargaining chips.

Constraints

A world in which regional and/or global nuclear arms racing was taking place would be subject to some constraints, in particular a lack of resources to engage in such activities. This would act as a brake on the proliferation of nuclear ordnance and delivery capabilities to smaller states. Economic constraints might also encourage the NWS and the *de facto* NWS to engage in arms control and non-proliferation negotiations in order to prevent economically crippling offensive and defensive arms races.

The existing technological and financial hurdles involved in making the transition from theoretical research to implementation are likely to continue to slow the proliferation of nuclear weapons beyond the existing NWS, and the *de facto* NWS. However, it is possible that even technologically and economically less developed states may be able to gain access to materials and technology following the collapse of a NWS or a *de facto* NWS.

It is also possible that new technological developments could act as a constraint on the emergence of a
high-salience nuclear future. For example, the evolution
of non-nuclear BMD in the US, and later in China,
might challenge assumptions about the utility of nuclear
weapons and conceptions of deterrence. On the other
hand, it could lead to a drive for more sophisticated
nuclear devices and their means of delivery. Moreover,
new conventional technologies are already beginning to
eclipse the military roles of nuclear ordnance and negate
some of the deterrent advantages claimed for the possession of nuclear weapons. This technological imper-
ative could become an important swing factor in the
future, provoking a move away from a high-salience
nuclear world to one dominated by sophisticated conventional weaponry and biological weapons, which are
cheaper and easier to produce, considered more 'usable'
and less vulnerable to detection.

B: A low-salience nuclear future

Characteristics

There are a number of possible low-salience nuclear
futures, ranging from a world in which national stocks
are reduced to hundreds rather than thousands of
nuclear weapons to a world of VNAs. Common to all
possibilities is the reduction in numbers of nuclear
weapons combined with a continuing commitment to
nuclear deterrence. Proponents of a low-salience nuclear
world stop short of advocating the total elimination of
nuclear weapons. In doing so, they overcome the
objections of those who argue that a NWFW is neither

desirable nor feasible because of the inability to destroy existing knowledge and the threat of nuclear breakout.

Although, until recently, trends indicated that a lower-salience nuclear world was the most likely, such a world may not be very stable or sustainable. Instead of resulting from purposeful and internationally agreed nuclear reduction policies, the shapers in movement towards a low-salience nuclear world may be those born of financial exigency or other unilateral decisions and factors that are driven by considerations other than security. But part of the explanation why such a world would always be susceptible to an upwards movement in warhead numbers stems from concerns about deployments of defensive systems or the emergence of threats from states developing new WMD capabilities and their delivery systems. Moreover, at present another mitigating factor is the lack of a credible concept of a multilateral balance of countervailing force in nuclear ordnance, delivery systems and defence systems between the relevant five to eight states.

It is possible, however, that a low-salience nuclear future could develop as a result of a planned process of reductions, rather than random and ad hoc decisions. Such a world might be less prone to instability and upward movement because it would be founded on a consensus that the world would be a safer place if nuclear weapons played a less visible role in international relations. In addition, it would be preceded by a rigorous analysis of the risks and pitfalls that might be encountered during the different disarmament stages, giving a greater chance for obstacles to be overcome. Advocates of low-salience futures have made a number of different suggestions as to how partial disarmament could be taken forward. Most proposals include a combination of, or a variation on, the following stages.

Stage One The NWS and the *de facto* NWS pledge to abandon any existing plans to modernize and upgrade their nuclear capabilities, move to implement the CTBT and a FMCT, and pledge their commitment to a strengthened and multilateral ABM Treaty. Political agreements are made to strengthen mechanisms to prevent the horizontal proliferation of nuclear weapons and delivery systems to additional states. This is facilitated by the provision of negative security assurances against nuclear threats, a commitment by all states to refrain from the use of conventional force not sanctioned by the UN, and the elimination of all non-strategic nuclear weapons by the NWS.

Stage Two An international nuclear deterrent force is established under UN Security Council auspices. This force is used principally for deterring hostile states by international agreement. During this stage, the commitment of the NWS and the *de facto* NWS to non-proliferation and multilateral disarmament is formalized in a new international security treaty. This includes 'No First Use' pledges by all eight states, and follows deep cuts in the nuclear arsenals of Russia and the US first to 2,000 and then to a maximum of 1,000 deployed warheads each. To facilitate these reductions, a strengthened system of safeguards and transparency measures is implemented.

Stage Three This stage (which many may regard as the final stage) sees movement to lower numbers by the US and Russia under an agreement that also brings China, France, the UK and the *de facto* NWS into negotiations. The objective of this stage is to reduce the number of deployed weapons of the NWS to a maximum of 200 each.

Stage Four Another stage, not always considered, is the introduction of VNAs. This process is largely concerned with operational status rather than numbers, leading to a low-salience nuclear future in which nuclear capabilities are retained only in disassembled form. This achieves some of the advantages of complete nuclear disarmament by removing all weapons from day-to-day operational status and thereby pushing them to the margins of political life. It also allows the current NWS to retain some of the core missions for nuclear forces by threatening to rebuild a few dozen weapons within a period of a few days or weeks. No international body would take possession of the weapons. Thus, a hybrid form of nuclear deterrence is retained, reducing fears associated with breakout while minimizing the risks associated with hair-trigger postures and accidental use.

The US and Russia have already begun to move in this direction by reducing the alert levels of portions of their nuclear arsenals. Proponents of this approach envisage a point at which the NWS would dismantle all assembled nuclear devices and place the resulting parts (including warheads, delivery vehicles and fissile materials) under bilateral, multilateral, and/or international monitoring and inspection. The weapon systems would be separated in such a way that any attempt to reassemble them could be verified. However, this approach would not involve a one-step process. In the early phases of transition, all the declared NWS might keep a reserve of operational nuclear weapons, perhaps a handful of submarines at sea or mobile missiles on land, or some combination of the two. Gradually, the operational readiness of these reserves could be reduced. For example, guidance sets could be removed from missiles at sea. Only at the final stage of this long process (which, it has been estimated, would take at least a decade and probably much longer), would the point be reached at which no nuclear weapon remained in assembled form and delivery systems were placed in a 'care and maintenance' status.

Advocates of VNAs argue that a form of nuclear deterrence would be retained under this version of a low-salience nuclear future. Former NWS would deter one another from reconstructing their nuclear arsenals with the threat to match such a move, and if two or more arsenals were ever reconstructed, the states holding them would deter each other from actual use by the same sort of deterrence that prevails today. A VNA regime would therefore require a clause allowing member states to withdraw from the agreement in order to reassemble part, or all, of their nuclear arsenal. The question of how much time would be required to achieve this reconstitution is critical. Whereas currently many nuclear weapons that have been taken off hair-trigger status could be re-targeted or reassembled in a matter of hours, a VNA regime would need to create a cushion of days or weeks, and eventually increase it to months. Moreover, to reduce fears about the consequences of breakout, the dismantled weapons would have to be stored in survivable, and thus possibly secret, locations in order to prevent any state from achieving a first-strike ability, and a certain number of submarines and mobile missiles would have to be kept operational.

Pressures

Economic factors may help induce a low-salience nuclear world as a result of the costs of maintaining and replacing nuclear ordnance. This is likely to be a crucial factor in the case of Russia, and may be an important determinant of exactly how low numbers will go in a low-salience nuclear world. For example, Moscow is at present judged incapable of maintaining its nuclear arsenal at current levels. Some suggest that Russia could possibly be left with a strategic arsenal of no more than 200–500 weapons by 2015. However, this unilateral, finance-led as opposed to norms-led approach to nuclear disarmament would fail to address the deep-rooted insecurities that many consider to be at the root of horizontal and vertical proliferation. The potential to reverse direction would therefore be an inevitable part of this process.

Increasing economic interdependence between the NWS, the *de facto* NWS and any nuclear aspirants would increase the incentives for planned and coordinated multilateral disarmament initiatives. The process of globalization may not remove political uncertainties from international relations, but it could continue to alter attitudes to security. This would not automatically result in a move down to zero, but it could lead states to assign greater importance to economic stability, making them more likely to accept and implement new security concepts and policies, including the development of more comprehensive global and regional arms management regimes. Again, although this would be preferable to ad hoc reductions, it would not necessarily result in a stable nuclear future unless it was accompanied by attempts to deal with the military and political motivations for proliferation.

Political cooperation is the swing factor that is most likely to produce the planned low-salience nuclear future envisaged by advocates of deep cuts and VNAs. Implementation of such actions is dependent on the evolution of a norms-led international political consensus in favour of disarmament. Such a consensus would be unlikely to emerge unless it were preceded by moves towards the creation of a more harmonious and cooperative international community. This would be aided by political developments, such as continued smooth evolution of power in Russia, allowing for the continuation of the government's commitment to maintain stability in Europe, cooperate with the West and build good relations with the US; improved relations between China, Russia and the US; and the emergence of a stronger UN that proved to be willing and able to act as the ultimate arbiter of regional conflicts.

Constraints

It may be difficult to build the confidence necessary to promote movement down to lower levels of nuclear weapons. Significant reductions are unlikely to occur in economically developed states unless systems are put in place which demonstrate tried and tested detection techniques and the effective handling of non-compliant situations. As the next section indicates, compliance and verification procedures are prone to political and technical difficulties that may take many years to resolve. This could hinder efforts to prevent a return to a high-salience nuclear world.

Progress towards a low-salience nuclear future will also be dependent on the establishment of effective arms control arrangements covering all states. Statements emanating from the NWS indicate that their policy-makers view the proliferation of WMD to hostile states as one of the most serious threats inherent in the post-Cold War strategic environment. The US has openly stated that it regards this threat as one of the fundamental contemporary justifications for its retention of nuclear weapons. Unless these fears can be allayed, military considerations are likely to negate disarmament initiatives, and the world may be pushed towards a situation where high nuclear postures are seen as necessary to counteract the insecurities generated by WMD proliferation.

Statements by the *de facto* NWS and some NPT NNWS show that there is a widespread belief that the existing nuclear non-proliferation regime is discriminatory and unsustainable. It is not easy to see how the NPT will ever be acceptable to the non-signatories, especially India, which views it as discriminatory and as a cloak for neo-imperialism. It may require the creation of a new treaty for this problem to be overcome, but judging by the time and effort expended on negotiations of the NPT, it is likely that such a comprehensive nuclear weapons convention would take many years to complete and be plagued by difficulties.

There are also a number of problems and constraints specifically related to the establishment of a VNA regime. Virtual arsenals could only be developed as a result of an extensive process of arms control stretching over many years. Optimistic predictions suggest that this could be achieved within a decade, but other estimates postulate a learning curve that could extend over three decades. During this period, the entire process could collapse as a result of a substantial growth in inter-state hostilities, perhaps resulting in greater instability.

A short-term problem is presented by the need to find acceptable transitional arrangements as the first steps towards the future establishment of a VNA regime. For the US and Russia this could, in theory, be quite straightforward. Nuclear warheads could be de-mated from their missiles, with 100–200 left as an operational reserve. The weapons could then be taken to a further stage of disassembly: fissile material and guidance sets could be removed and stored separately. However, this process is likely to be more problematic for the UK and France. The latter has retained nuclear missile sub-marines as its dominant nuclear capability and deterrent against a surprise first strike; for the UK they are the only deterrent. This raises the question of whether it would be possible to find a way of retaining the deterrent effect of sea-based forces and to verify the status of such weapons. It is feasible that the first of these hurdles

81

could be overcome if the guidance sets were to be removed from the missiles and stored where they could be rapidly retrieved for reinsertion in the missiles. Furthermore, it has been suggested that the second hurdle could be overcome if submarines, missiles and warheads were tagged for identification, and if each side could request a random surfacing for examination of the missiles, though the practicality of this must be in doubt. Despite these suggestions, it is apparent that these issues could present major difficulties for the architects of any virtual deterrence regime.

There are also significant differences of opinion over the impact of BMD deployment on virtual arsenals. While some have argued that missile defences could have a stabilizing effect on a VNA regime (by deterring aggressor states considering breakout), a number of potential drawbacks have also been identified. Such defences may be ineffective against certain forms of attack and may foment rather than curtail instability. In this regard, it is possible to envisage a situation whereby a combination of rapid breakout from the VNA agreement and strategic defence would prove highly destabilizing in the early stages of reconstitution of a nuclear force.

Verification of virtual arsenals would also present a problem, requiring a significant upgrading of the staff and powers of the IAEA, or the creation of an alternative organization. Such an agency would need to verify both the provisions of the dismantling agreement and the non-diversion of civilian nuclear material for a clandestine nuclear weapons programme. The agency would need powers of short-notice inspection and would have to monitor key nuclear-weapons-related facilities on a continuous basis, not only in the declared NWS but also in threshold and aspirant NWS. It is questionable, moreover, whether all states would be willing to subject themselves to such tough and intrusive verification measures and provide the resources required to implement them.

The issue of whether a world of VNAs would be more or less stable (i.e. more or less war-prone) than a world of assembled nuclear weapons currently provokes considerable debate in the open literature. A number of potential flaws in the regime could give rise to serious instability. First, asymmetries in reaction times could emerge, allowing one state to reconstitute its forces more rapidly and thereby gain a strategic advantage. This could become a problem, in particular if reconstitution were easier and quicker in an authoritarian state than in a democracy. Second, a policy of trying to create a VNA regime might suggest that possession of a virtual arsenal was acceptable, leading to the proliferation of such capabilities. Third, there is a possibility that moves towards the establishment of virtual arsenals in the US and Russia could undermine the security of those states that are protected by extended nuclear deterrence guarantees. This could lead such states to seek more independent means of defence, including nuclear and biological weapons.

C: A nuclear-weapon-free world

Characteristics

A NWFW would be one in which nuclear weapons are no longer instruments of state policy. The weapons would be eliminated under a system of international control, possibly involving the creation of an international force under UN Security Council auspices. Such a world might contain the following necessary components:

- a universal global political agreement not to possess nuclear ordnance;

- the verified disarmament of existing weapons and their delivery systems, and a verified commitment not to construct new ones;

- the placing of all fissile materials within states under IAEA safeguards; and

- a mechanism for dealing with non-compliance with, and breakout from, zero.

As was realized in both the Intermediate-Range Nuclear Forces (INF) and CTBT negotiations, zero may be the only basis for a negotiation that seeks to achieve a situation of long-term stability in nuclear weapon deployments. This is partly because compliance with such an agreement will be easier to verify than any global freeze in numbers or reduction in activities. However, such negotiations may not be feasible without involving parallel developments in regimes covering potential delivery systems and other WMD, as well as conventional force levels and deployments. It will also be necessary to go into such negotiations with a much clearer idea of what constitutes zero nuclear weapons, or a disarmed world, than currently exists.

In order to reach a NWFW, the world may first have to go through a stage where nuclear arsenals are replaced with VNAs, whereby warheads, fissile materials and delivery vehicles are placed at different safe storage sites, each of which is subject to monitoring and inspection. Such a regime may bolster the confidence of states reluctant to relinquish their nuclear capabilities entirely because they fear the threat of breakout. Despite the possibilities for regression to a higher-salience nuclear world that are inherent in VNAs, this semi-disarmed world might be all that is achievable until confidence in a move to zero can be assured.

Pressures

A NWFW might be produced by a traumatic event. Such a shock could be the purposeful use of nuclear weapons by a state, thus breaking the unambiguous but informal taboo against actual use (as opposed to threat of use) that has existed since 1945. Another potential shock event could be the unintended use of nuclear weapons following a nuclear accident or unauthorized actions. Either of these scenarios might provoke a sudden backlash against nuclear weapons by mass opinion and at policy-making levels. This might generate the considerable shift in political will and public opinion that would be necessary to bring about a rapid move to zero. Other factors conducive to a steady move towards zero might include:

- the continued development of regional structures and institutions, including the establishment of a highly institutionalized, legitimate and universally accepted mechanism to resolve conflicts;
- changes in global attitudes towards security and the role of nuclear weapons within it, including an international consensus over the benefits of a NWFW; and
- increased confidence in international arms management regimes through greater transparency and the strengthening of verification and non-compliance activities.

Economic and political incentives may also influence unilateral or multilateral steps by the NWS from a minimum nuclear deterrent to a recessed deterrent. Between 2010 and 2020, both France and the UK will face the question of whether or not to replace their nuclear arsenals. Policy responses are like to depend primarily on threat perceptions combined with their confidence in compliance and verification procedures. However, such decisions could also be swayed by issues such as the cost of, and public support for, replacement.

Constraints

The development of a NWFW is likely to be a difficult enterprise, more so than it was during previous efforts between 1945 and 1964. Fifty years of relatively unconstrained nuclear arming presents the international community with significant practical difficulties if a move to zero is envisaged. This is not just because the number of states likely to be involved is greater, but also because nuclear energy technology is more advanced, more fissile material has been produced, and the means of delivery for nuclear ordnance have become more diversified.

Universality of commitment to zero nuclear weapons would be difficult to achieve, as it would involve the NWS conducting multilateral negotiations over reductions in weapon numbers, and engaging India, Israel and Pakistan in this process without weakening the existing NPT regime. The latter may prove more problematic than the former, if only because the NWS are under a legal obligation contained within the NPT to discuss the issue 'in good faith', whereas at present the *de facto* NWS are not. India, Israel and Pakistan may also be more reluctant than the NWS to engage in such discussions than the NWS because they, like other potential proliferators, are in situations of acute regional conflict.

The practical issues associated with dismantling all nuclear arsenals are likely to be considerable. For example, once the nuclear weapons are disassembled, it will be extremely difficult to account for the destruction of dual-use components or their use in other roles. Thus the degree of dismantling, the disposal of components and the destruction of manufacturing facilities will all generate uncertainties over what constitutes a NWFW, and how to maintain such an environment once it has been achieved.

The destruction of delivery systems is also unlikely to be straightforward. Some delivery vehicles, such as cruise missiles and strike aircraft, have well-developed roles in the delivery of conventional ordnance. Others, such as ballistic missiles, might be regarded as having legitimate roles if they were to be fitted with conventional warheads or used as satellite launchers. A control regime covering missiles would therefore have to accompany any move to zero, despite the complications posed by the dual-use nature of many of the technologies involved.

Missile defence systems also present difficulties for any move to zero. On the one hand, these systems could drive numbers of offensive nuclear systems upwards if deployed before zero is attained, and they may also be perceived as strengthening the position of states wishing to break out from any arms control arrangement in the early stages of such an activity. On the other hand, they may deter any move away from zero once it has been achieved because they could handle limited attacks.

A non-nuclear world would maximize US conventional military superiority. Through its advanced technologies and pursuit of the RMA, the US now has, and will retain for some years, a substantial degree of dominance in the field of conventional warfare. This situation could affect the evolution of a NWFW in different ways. Although it might encourage further moves towards zero, and attempts to stay there, by Washington's traditional allies, the prospect of conventional asymmetry could increase incentives to break out among its adversaries. Moreover, it may encourage less advanced states to develop biological, chemical, or even nuclear weapons to compensate for their conventional inferiority. This suggests that, in order to achieve and maintain zero, a system will be required to minimize conventional threats and resolve political differences without resort to warfare.

The existence of large global stockpiles of weapons-grade fissile materials, arising both from nuclear weapon programmes and from civil reprocessing activities, creates a situation where re-weaponization by the NWS and weaponization by several NNWS could for many decades take place in a relatively short time-frame. There are significant technical difficulties and economic costs involved in ensuring that such materials can never be used in weapons again. This is particularly true of plutonium, which can only be disposed of either by burning it in reactors as mixed oxide (MOX) fuel or by immobilizing it with high-level waste in glass or ceramic form and placing it in permanent underground storage. Currently, the burning of excess plutonium as MOX fuel in power reactors attracts little support, not least because of the cost of MOX fabrication. Moreover, the option of storing it under national or international control still leaves open the possibility of this material being diverted or stolen by state or terrorist agents. This implies that a necessary part of moving to zero may be agreement on and implementation of an effective system for immobilizing or de-naturing weapons-grade plutonium, or at least reducing it to the used-fuel standard, as well as an enhanced system of management of plutonium in civil fuel cycles.

It is inconceivable that states will accept a world of zero nuclear weapons in the absence of a strong and transparent system for handling allegations of non-compliance and for acting against attempts at break out from it. The handling by the UN Security Council of the alleged activities of the DPRK and Iraq indicate the difficulties inherent in creating mechanisms to undertake these tasks.

It is not self-evident in the short term that a world of zero nuclear weapons would be significantly different in qualitative terms from one of deployed nuclear weapons. In the immediate aftermath of arriving at zero, conceptions of deterrence associated with nuclear weapons might well continue to operate. It could be argued that a minimum deterrent stretches beyond the ambiguity inherent in unsafeguarded research and power reactors and reprocessing and enrichment plants to include the existence of both fissile materials under national jurisdiction and physical control, and the necessary technological skills and facilities to manufacture nuclear devices and their means of delivery. The former capabilities have been labelled by some analysts as situations of recessed or non-weaponized deterrence.

It is unclear how long such capabilities would continue to have a deterrent effect in the situation of zero nuclear weapons, given arguments about the rapid loss of the tacit knowledge required to manufacture nuclear devices and the difficulties of re-manufacturing nuclear weapon designs without access to explosive testing. However, it might be argued that a world of zero nuclear weapons would, for several years, *de facto* be a partially disarmed one, in which the differences between states would reside in the time they needed to reconstitute a minimum nuclear force.

Regional nuclear salience

This discussion has highlighted the problems that are likely to confront the architects of global nuclear disarmament if they are to seek to prevent high salience and encourage movement towards a lower-salience nuclear future. However, one major difficulty that remains to be addressed, and that complicates the situation further, is regional nuclear salience. The international environment is more complex than the descriptions of abstract nuclear futures sketched out above would suggest. Different parts of the world are moving at different rates towards lower nuclear salience, and it appears that some regions are going in the opposite direction. One potential development over the next 20 to 30 years, therefore, is the uneasy coexistence of high- and low-salience regions.

A number of regions have already moved in the direction of a NWFW, pushing nuclear weapons to the margins of regional politics. South America, Africa, and Southeast Asia now embrace a non-nuclear-weapon stance and are active in pressuring the NWS and *de facto* NWS to follow suit. The emergence of another NWFZ in Central Asia also appears imminent.

In Europe, France and the UK no longer envisage specific traditional war-fighting roles for nuclear ordnance. Both states claim to have a minimum deterrent, which suggests that their next step towards disarmament would involve either the merging of their capabilities into a European nuclear force or steps towards the creation of virtual arsenals. However, it is possible that French and UK membership of NATO may act as one of the constraints preventing such moves, in particular as the new Strategic Concept reinforces the role of nuclear weapons in deterring unconventional threats from states hostile to the West.

Though the US and Russia have been reducing warhead numbers and have removed part of their arsenals from hair-trigger operational status, the nuclear doctrines of both states indicate that they continue to envisage a military role for nuclear ordnance. Economic and political pressures are likely to continue to force numbers downwards over the next decade, at least until START III levels are reached, but this will not necessarily be indicative of a change in attitudes to nuclear weapons. At some point over the next two decades, advances in US conventional capabilities may alter this situation, leading the US to consider moves towards lower nuclear salience and Russia to rely more heavily on its nuclear capability.

In the Middle East, Northeast Asia and South Asia, the trend appears to be towards higher nuclear salience. These regions suffer high levels of political instability, which increases the appeal of nuclear weapons and other forms of WMD to fulfil military and political roles. Unless regional tensions can be eased and disputes settled, missile proliferation in these areas is likely to continue, and a new era of nuclear arms racing may occur.

Conclusions

The existence of disparities between geographic areas of high and low salience is likely to create the potential for retrograde steps in the regions where disarmament has been moving forward. One way to help prevent this outcome would be for policy-makers to take a contextual approach to security – one that emphasizes and attempts to understand the regional context of nuclear behaviour. Such an approach would encourage questions to be raised over what the notion of nuclear stability means in different areas of the world, and how it could be achieved. This issue is often discussed in a broad, ill-defined sense, on the assumption that what constitutes and creates stability in one region is likely to be applicable elsewhere. What is needed is a greater understanding of the different confidence- and security-building measures that would reduce threat perceptions in different regions, and prevent regional and global arms races in offensive and defensive conventional and nuclear weaponry.

PART III

STABILIZING AND SECURING THE FUTURE NUCLEAR ENVIRONMENT

Introduction

The analysis in Part II has revealed the complexities and difficulties involved in creating and maintaining global and regional stability in each of the nuclear futures that appear possible. Although it suggests that none of these futures can offer permanent, guaranteed peace and stability, it is possible to order them on the basis of their potential for achieving and sustaining a safer world. The clearest conclusion to be drawn is that a world dominated by high nuclear salience presents the most serious threat to international security. This salience could either be a product of a global restructuring of international relationships into a new multi-dimensional pattern or result from instabilities and competitive arming in one or more regions. This could lead to many states taking military measures to try to sustain their security, including both enhancing their capabilities in the area of offensive nuclear forces and/or deploying missile defences. Dealing with such a situation is likely to confront policy-makers with high degrees of complexity and uncertainty, and many are likely to seek means to avert such a situation.

Assessing which of the other nuclear futures examined in this study – a NWFW or a low-salience nuclear world – is likely to generate a more stable and secure nuclear environment is an even more complex task. One significant difference between them is that the reductions in nuclear salience witnessed in the mid–1990s were shaped by perceptions of reductions in threat, economic pressures and other contextual factors, rather than necessarily by conscious national commitments towards such a world. For a NWFW implies a significant change in contemporary international attitudes towards nuclear weaponry. However, it is feasible that the evolution of verification technology and compliance procedures could eventually generate increasing confidence in the ability of a NWFW to deal with potential violators of a disarmament regime, and thus make it a more attractive policy choice. For in a world or region where nuclear weapons play an overt role, whether high- or low-profile, threat perceptions are always likely to remain significant. It thus seems conceivable that a low-salience nuclear world, including a world of VNAs, may continue to be prone to greater instability than a NWFW, and contain pressures to move towards high salience.

Given this situation, it could be a mistake to regard the creation of a low-salience nuclear future as the ultimate objective of arms control and disarmament initiatives. While low salience may be seen as a valuable stepping stone and short- to medium-term goal, the case for pursuing the long-term elimination of nuclear weapons is compelling. The problem, as ever, is how to reach this position without generating self-defeating instabilities on the way, a subject which is beyond the limited scope of this study, but one which merits future examination. The more immediate contemporary question is what steps might be taken to reverse trends towards a high-salience nuclear future and promote a low-salience one, and thus assist in developing measures that could eventually lead to a NWFW. Numerous initiatives could be proposed, and it is convenient to examine them from two perspectives: diplomatic activities, and arms control and disarmament initiatives.

Diplomatic activities

There are several activities and contexts that may assist the international community to shape a safer nuclear future. Some are related to the developing strategic nuclear relationships outlined in this study and are predicated on attempting to reduce threat perceptions among the key actors, especially where the introduction of new technologies may exacerbate them. Others are more specifically directed at the regional context, where the main variable is likely to be whether long-standing disputes can be overcome. All these activities may well be dependent, however, on whether the international community can embrace more collective, cooperative notions of security in the future.

A broader dialogue of missile defences and their impact on strategic stability

The US is currently engaged in development work and feasibility studies for both a NMD and a TMD, and appears to be on the point of deciding whether to deploy the former. If such defences are deployed, in the US and possibly elsewhere, the effects on future strategic relationships could be far-reaching. During the Cold

War, the debate on missile defences emphasized their destabilizing consequences in precipitating an action–reaction strategic armaments competition between offensive and defensive forces. This, essentially, was the rationale underpinning the ABM Treaty agreed in the early 1970s. Today, the emerging international context is different and some have argued that the deployment of missile defences may enhance, rather than undermine, strategic stability.

What this suggests is that there is a need for a broader dialogue on the potential impact of missile defences on the future nuclear environment. This could assist both in clarifying particular national positions on missile defences and in identifying the areas of critical disagreement where innovative and constructive thinking may be needed. This dialogue may also have to embrace competing conceptions of deterrence, the relationship between nuclear, chemical and biological weapons, and regional differences in nuclear posture. This type of dialogue is important in developing common understandings on nuclear deterrence and in reducing the possibilities for accidental or unintentional nuclear use.

A European dialogue

At present, there are differences of opinion within the EU over the future role of nuclear weapons, particularly between the former Cold War neutrals (Austria, Ireland and Sweden) and the NATO states. However, this is a region where there has been a move from high- to low-salience policies over nuclear weaponry in the past decade. This is not to discount the existence of Russia's nuclear capability and its impact on threat perceptions and the possibility that another state outside the region might pose a WMD challenge at some point in the future.

The elements of a dialogue within this region might focus on ways of preventing the emergence of a high-salience world; a consideration of what would constitute nuclear sufficiency for the UK, France and Europe as a whole during an interim disarmament process; the steps through which global nuclear disarmament might be achieved and the forums for their negotiation; and the role that missile defences might or might not play in this process.

A South Asian dialogue

The India–Pakistan nuclear relationship currently lacks the agreed rules and understandings that were developed with great difficulty between the US and the former Soviet Union during the Cold War. There is considerable unease outside the region that this may lead to a breach of the taboo on the actual use of nuclear weapons that has been preserved since 1945. This is in part because, unlike the US and the Soviet Union, the two states have a long common border, have engaged in three conventional wars, and each feels its territorial and state integrity is threatened by the other.

Since 1998, there has thus been a desire outside the region to foster a constructive dialogue on the nuclear future between India and Pakistan, although the measures through which this might be accomplished have so far proved far from straightforward and any future initiatives may be seen by the two states as unwarranted interference. There is also the added complication that any initiatives by states or organizations from outside the region could push the two states towards further nuclearization. One justification for continued efforts is the desire to help prevent a hasty or inadvertent resort to the use of nuclear weapons during a military crisis involving both states.

A Northeast Asian dialogue

Northeast Asia is another region where nuclear weapon issues are increasing in salience. It contains China, a NWS; the DPRK, a state that continues to resist efforts to introduce greater transparency over its nuclear programme and that has a developing ballistic missile capability; Japan and the Republic of Korea (RoK), two states that are at the forefront of the global economy, have advanced nuclear energy and missile capabilities and consider themselves to be under threat from neighbouring states; and finally Taiwan, which possesses similar attributes.

While at present the region seems likely to remain in a cycle of nuclear uncertainty, recent moves to re-establish the High Level meetings between the RoK and the DPRK indicate that dialogue on sensitive issues is possible. The historical record also suggests that US security guarantees have played a major role in stemming desires for indigenous nuclear capabilities in the region. Assuming the US is prepared to continue with these arrangements, they could provide a platform for further discussion over a future regional security arrangement and how it might be brought to fruition. One element of doubt inevitably relates to whether the US and China will be able to reconcile their differences, not least over the rights of NNWS in the region to deploy TMD.

The search for further Middle East dialogue

The Middle East also represents a region where there is a potential for heightened nuclear salience, but this does not mean that such a trend is inevitable. Efforts to deal with the situation in the past have focused on the Oslo peace process and on the establishment of a Zone Free of Weapons of Mass Destruction (ZFWMD), which would embrace any chemical and biological weapons capabilities in the region. Whatever judgment is made about the progress of both initiatives, they seem set to continue to provide the platform for dealing with the residual nuclear issue. What remains unclear is whether a failure of either the peace process or the ZFWMD, or both, would precipitate the withdrawal of Israel's neighbours from the NPT. Such actions would be likely to generate fears about their future nuclear intentions, leading to a higher nuclear salience in the region as a whole. Added uncertainty also stems from the situation in Iraq and doubts about whether the new arrangement for verification and monitoring of its potential WMD capabilities under the terms of UN Security Council resolutions can be implemented.

Other regional dialogues

One very positive development in the past decade has been the increase in the number of regions opting to negotiate agreements committing their members to forgo the ownership of nuclear weapons and the deployment of other states' weapons on their territories. Africa, Southeast Asia and Latin America and the Caribbean now fall into this category of nuclear-weapon-free regions, thus accentuating the trend towards a differentiated and asymmetrical nuclear-weapon world. Ensuring that these zones engender confidence and political support among their respective state parties, and that the NWS assist in this process, will be a continuing diplomatic task.

Arms control and disarmament initiatives

While diplomatic activities seek to address the underlying causes of inter-state conflict, arms control and disarmament initiatives aim at reducing nuclear dangers by constraining the numbers and types of nuclear armaments possessed by states. In current circumstances, the major needs in this area appear to be to strengthen existing treaties and regimes, and to develop new activities that could increase the chances of 'holding the line' following the deterioration in relations between the US, Russia and China.

A dialogue among the five NWS recognized by the NPT

Movement towards reduced warhead numbers globally is not likely unless the five NWS collectively can agree on how to undertake this. Not only is this a necessary condition for sustaining arms control and moving forward with further disarmament; there is also now a question mark over how these states should address other *de facto* nuclear capabilities. Central to this situation will be the momentum generated within the US–Russia START process.

Following Moscow's decision to expand its arsenal of tactical nuclear weapons to compensate for conventional weaknesses, the issue of how to deal with tactical nuclear ordnance may also need to receive more attention. Until now, only the strategic forces of the US and Russia have been covered by START. Any future negotiations involving all five NWS will necessitate a move from START to a Nuclear Arms Reduction Treaty (NART) – that is, a treaty reducing all nuclear weapons, strategic and tactical. The question of how Russia could be encouraged to engage in such negotiations is likely to be problematical, especially in the context of US developments in precision weapons and the debate over NMD. Demands that reductions in Russian tactical weapons should be balanced by constraints on US precision-guided ordnance would present major difficulties for NATO states. Moreover, although such a treaty would ideally also include China, France and the UK, Beijing is unlikely to cooperate unless offered significant incentives. These obstacles could feasibly be overcome through dialogue between the NWS, which will need to address the issue of threat perceptions and the question of what kinds of confidence- and security-building measures might influence them. In the absence of dialogue, it is likely that the arms control agenda will stagnate, confidence in existing arrangements will erode, and states will seek security through unilateral actions.

A possible review of US and Russian nuclear alert status

Owing to the nature of their strategic nuclear relationship, both Moscow and Washington keep several nuclear systems on high states of alert readiness. But this situation places stress on the continued reliability of nuclear command and control procedures. Whether these states will consider the possibilities for reducing some or all of their weapon systems from such an alert status will obviously depend on the context in which their relationship evolves. However, if some initiatives to move towards a more relaxed nuclear posture could be adopted, there is good reason to assume that these would be received in a very favourable light by the rest of the international community.

NATO's policy on No First Use

The Washington Summit Communiqué stated NATO's intention to establish a mechanism to review its First Use options and to consider a policy of No First Use. Such a policy might possibly reduce Russian and Chinese threat perceptions, and thereby improve the chances for movement towards a lower-salience nuclear future.

Ratification of the CTBT

The CTBT bans all nuclear test explosions and would help curb the development of new designs of nuclear weapons and make more difficult the production of modified delivery systems. It could help check a potential nuclear arms race in South Asia, as well as any renewed Chinese–Russian–US nuclear arms competition. Entry into force of the CTBT would be a significant step in any strategy to prevent further horizontal and vertical nuclear proliferation.

Strengthening the NPT

It is vital that the NPT and its associated arrangements should not be weakened, as this treaty is the linchpin of the global nuclear non-proliferation regime. To avoid this outcome, two issues need addressing. First, how can the parties to the NPT ease the tensions arising from the nature of the Treaty, in particular India's long-standing complaint that it discriminates against the NNWS? An additional complication in dealing with this question is that any recognition of India and Pakistan as NWS in the light of their May 1998 tests would set a dangerous precedent for further nuclear proliferation. One solution to this problem would be for the NWS to reinvigorate their commitment to eventual nuclear weapon elimination and thereby, over time, seek to secure India's and Pakistan's cooperation with global non-proliferation efforts.

Second, how can disagreements over which of the NPT's objectives should take precedence be resolved? A helpful step towards this goal would be to clarify the decision on Strengthening the Review Process and in taking steps to implement the Principles and Objectives for Nuclear Non-Proliferation and Disarmament document adopted at the 1995 NPT Review and Extension Conference, as since that time both have been the subject of many interpretations.

Strengthening the CWC and the BTWC

Given the intense insecurity generated by fears over the proliferation and potential use of chemical and biological weapons, it is important that the Chemical Weapons Convention and the Bacteriological and Toxins Weapons Convention are strengthened if nuclear disarmament is ever to become a realistic possibility. One of the problems for which solutions will need to be found is the issue of how to detect non-compliance. The verification arrangements of the CWC have provided a basis for establishing criteria in this area, but even these may need bolstering in the future. Similarly, in the context of the BTWC, there continues to be concern that scientific advances will make biological weapons easier to acquire. The negotiation of a verification protocol for the BTWC has gone some way to addressing many of the crucial issues, but this area is likely to remain one of concern until the international community finds an appropriate means for dealing with cases of material breaches or other non-compliance activities. Nuclear disarmament efforts are therefore likely to be hampered until such methods for dealing with these other types of WMD are found.

Furthering FMCT negotiations

A FMCT would constitute a significant step in dealing with the dangers posed by fissile materials, as well as one of the building blocks for a fissile-material-led disarmament process. A priority for the UK, France and the US must be to reach a compromise over the issue of fissile material production and stocks on the one hand,

and nuclear disarmament (the nominal issue that is blocking progress in negotiations in the CD) on the other, and to engage Russia and China in constructive negotiations on these matters. Transparency in this area would help reduce threat perceptions and may convince the NNWS that the NWS are genuinely committed to moving the arms control and disarmament process forward.

Addressing restrictions on delivery systems

Currently, there is no multinational negotiation or treaty dealing with WMD delivery systems. Rather, the restrictions that exist are imposed through the Missile Technology Control Regime (MTCR), which has drawn up export guidelines for supplier states. Suggestions have been made in the past for negotiated limitations on WMD delivery systems, but have encountered at least three major problems: the desire of existing NWS to retain their freedom to develop, transfer and acquire such systems; the question of whether constraints should be placed on offensive systems only, or both offensive and defensive systems; and the issue of their use as satellite launchers. This combination of two classes of states and problems of dual-use suggests that any treaty would be very similar in structure to the NPT, whose discriminatory nature remains unacceptable in principle to many NNWS.

At the same time, it should be noted that existing bilateral nuclear arms control arrangements between Russia and the US are almost all focused upon constraints on delivery systems, rather than on nuclear ordnance. It may also be the case that this is the most difficult aspect of procuring a nuclear deterrent capability. It might therefore be appropriate to revisit the issue of moving beyond the MTCR and the Intermediate Nuclear Forces (INF) Treaty to examine the possibilities to forge agreements banning the procurement of specific types of delivery systems.

Alternative nuclear futures: some conclusions

This study's most significant contribution to future debates over nuclear weaponry probably lies in the questions it has raised about the nuclear present and the alternative nuclear futures it has identified. One conclusion that may be derived from it is that several new problems and issues are emerging in the nuclear elements of the international security environment. The first category of issue concerns the relationship between the nuclear future and developments in conventional weaponry, missile defences and biological weapons. Although this study has given some indication of the possible effects of developments in these technologies, the question of what would happen if current efforts to control the spread of WMD and delivery vehicles fail remains problematic. Would the result be the rapid proliferation of such weapons, or the slow spread envisaged by some analysts? Would states resort to national responses to this situation, or would it be possible to build a new consensus to prevent this outcome?

The second category of issues concerns regional discontinuities, asymmetrical deterrence and competing deterrence conceptions. As this study has shown, it is a subject that requires urgent attention if a return to a high-salience world, different in form from that experienced between 1945 and 1989, is to be avoided. The third and fourth categories of issues relate respectively to the political and technical hurdles associated with arms control and disarmament. Foremost among these are the issues of compliance and verification.

A move towards a new high-salience nuclear future is not inevitable, but unless positive steps are taken by the international community to prevent it, such an outcome may happen. The steps required appear to be of two types: those to prevent nuclear weaponry from dominating strategic doctrines; and those to prevent current regional conflicts becoming nuclear ones. The first of these steps is likely to require constructive dialogue on a range of issues that may affect future threat perceptions and strategic stability in both the regional and the global context; the second relates to the broader evolving international environment and the role that collective measures, such as multilateral arms control and confidence-building, might have in engendering security within it. Positive developments in both these areas will be needed to provide a context that enables progress to be made towards promoting and sustaining a lower-salience nuclear world and to make consideration of a world without deployed nuclear weapons a realizable goal.

BIBLIOGRAPHY

Books

Adams, B. D., *Ballistic Missile Defense*, American Elsevier Publishers, 1971.

Adler, E. and Barnett, M., eds, *Security Communities*, Cambridge, Cambridge University Press, 1998.

Ahmed, S. and Cortright, D., eds, *Pakistan and the Bomb*, Notre Dame, Ind., University of Notre Dame Press, 1998.

Allison, G. T., Coté, O. R., Falkenrath, R. A. and Miller, S. E., *Avoiding Nuclear Anarchy: Containing the Threat of Loose Russian Nuclear Weapons and Fissile Material*, Cambridge, Mass., The MIT Press, 1996.

Arnett E., ed., *Nuclear Weapons After the Comprehensive Test Ban: Implications for Modernization and Proliferation*, Oxford, Oxford University Press for SIPRI, 1996.

Asahi Shimbun, *The Road to the Abolition of Nuclear Weapons*, Tokyo, April 1999.

Bailey, K. C., *Doomsday Weapons in the Hands of Many: The Arms Control Challenge of the 90's*, Urbana, Ill., University of Illinois Press, 1991.

Bailey, K. C., ed., *Weapons of Mass Destruction: Costs Versus Benefits*, Dhaka, Manohar Publishers, 1996.

Barnaby F., *The Role and Control of Weapons in the 1990s*, London, Routledge, 1992.

Baylis, J. and O'Neill, R. O., eds, *Alternative Nuclear Futures: The Role of Nuclear Weapons in the Post-Cold War World*, Oxford, Oxford University Press, 1999.

Blacker, C. D. and Duffy, G., eds, *International Arms Control. Issues and Agreements*, 2nd edn, Stanford, Calif., Stanford University Press, 1984.

Blair, B. G., *The Logic of Accidental Nuclear War*, Washington, DC, Brookings Institution, 1993.

Booth, K., ed., *Statecraft and Security: The Cold War and Beyond*,

Cambridge, Cambridge University Press, 1998.

Bowen, W. Q., *The Politics of Ballistic Missile Nonproliferation*, London, Macmillan, 2000.

Brown, J., ed., *New Horizons and New Strategies in Arms Control*, Albuquerque, N. Mex., Sandia National Laboratories, 1998.

Brown, M., Lynn-Jones, S. and Miller, S. eds, *The Perils of Anarchy: Contemporary Realism and International Security*, Cambridge, Mass., The MIT Press, 1995.

Bundy, M., Crowe, W. J. and Drell, S., *Reducing Nuclear Danger: The Road Away from the Brink*, New York, Council on Foreign Relations Press, 1993.

Buzan, B., *People, States and Fear*, Harvester Wheatsheaf, 1991.

Buzan, B. and Herring, E., *The Arms Dynamic in World Politics*, London, Lynne Rienner, 1998.

Chari, P. R., Cheema, P. I. and Iftekharuzzaman, I, eds, *Nuclear Nonproliferation in India and Pakistan: South Asian Perspectives*, Dhaka, Manohar Publishers, 1996.

Cimbala, S. J., *The Past and Future of Nuclear Deterrence*, London, Praeger, 1998.

Clarke, M. ed., *New Perspectives on Security*, London, Brassey's, 1995.

Couloumbis, T. and Dokos, T., *Arms Control and Security in the Middle East and the CIS Republics*, Athens, Hellenic Foundation for European and Foreign Policy, 1995.

van Creveld, M., *Nuclear Proliferation and the Future of Conflict*, New York, Free Press, 1993.

Croft, S., *Strategies of Arms Control*, Manchester, Manchester University Press, 1996.

Croft, S. and Terriff, T. eds, *Critical Reflections on Security and Change*, London, Frank Cass, 2000.

Dando, M., *Biological Warfare in the 21st Century*, London, Brassey's, 1994.

Fischer, D., *Stopping the Spread of Nuclear Weapons: The Past and the Prospects*, London, Routledge, 1992.

Fischer, D., Kotter, W. and Müller, H., *Nuclear Non-Proliferation and Global Order*, Oxford, Oxford University Press for SIPRI, 1994.

Freedman, L., *The Evolution of Nuclear Strategy*, London, Macmillan, 1983.

Gardner, G. T., *Nuclear Nonproliferation. A Primer*, London, Lynne Rienner, 1994.

Goldblat, J., *Arms Control: A Guide to Negotiations and Agreements*, London, Sage Publications, 1996.

Goodpaster, A. J., *Further Reins on Nuclear Arms*, Washington, DC, Atlantic Council, 1993.

Gray, C. S., *The Second Nuclear Age*, London, Lynne Rienner, 1999.

Huntington, S., *The Clash of Civilizations and the Remaking of World Order*, New York, Simon and Schuster, 1996.

Job, B. ed., *The Insecurity Dilemma. National Security of Third World States*, London, Lynne Rienner, 1992.

Jones, R. W. and McDonough, M. G. with Dalton, T. F. and Koblentz, G. D., *Tracking Nuclear Proliferation 1998*, Washington, DC, Carnegie Endowment for International Peace, 1998.

Karem, M., *A Nuclear-Weapon-Free Zone in the Middle East*, New York, Greenwood Press, 1988.

Karp, A., *Ballistic Missile Proliferation: The Politics and Technics*, Oxford, Oxford University Press for SIPRI, 1996.

Katzenstein, P., ed., *The Culture of National Security*, New York, Columbia University Press, 1996

Kemp, G. and Stahl, S., eds, *Arms Control and Weapons Proliferation in the Middle East and South Asia*, New York, St Martin's Press, 1992.

Krause, K. and Williams M. C., eds, *Critical Security Studies: Concepts and Cases*, London, UCL Press, 1997.

Larsen, J. and Rattray, G., *Arms Control: Toward the 21st Century*, London, Lynne Rienner, 1996.

Lodgaard, S. and Pfaltzgraff, R., eds, *Arms and Technology Transfers: Security and Economic Considerations Among Importing and Exporting States*, Geneva, United Nations Institute for Disarmament Research, 1995.

Lynn-Jones, S. and Miller, S., eds, *Global Dangers: Changing Dimensions of International Security*, Cambridge, Mass., MIT Press, 1995.

Mack A., ed., *Nuclear Policies in Northeast Asia*, Geneva, United Nations Institute for Disarmament Research, 1995.

Mazarr, M. J., ed., *Nuclear Weapons in a Transformed World. The Challenge of Virtual Nuclear Arsenals*, London, Macmillan, 1997.

111

Nair, V. K., *Nuclear India*, New Delhi, Lancer International, 1992.

Nolan, J., *Trappings of Power: Ballistic Missiles in the Third World*, Washington, DC, Brookings Institution, 1991.

Nye, J., *Understanding International Conflict*, New York, Harper-Collins, 1993.

Office of Technology Assessment, US Congress, *Dismantling the Bomb and Managing the Nuclear Materials*, Washington, DC, US Government Printing Office, September 1993.

Patman, R. C., ed., *Security in a Post-Cold War World*, London, Macmillan, 1999.

Paul, T. V., Harknett R. and Wirtz J. J., eds, *The Absolute Weapon Revisited: Nuclear Arms and the Emerging International Order*, Ann Arbour, The University of Michigan Press, 1998.

Perkovich, G., *India's Nuclear Bomb: The Impact on Global Proliferation*, Berkeley, California, University of California Press, 1999.

Poole, J. B., and Guthrie, R. eds, *Verification 1996 – Arms Control, Peacekeeping and the Environment*, Boulder, Colo., Westview Press, 1996.

Rotblat, J., Steinberger, J. and Udgaonkar, B., eds, *A Nuclear-Weapon-Free World: Desirable? Feasible?*, Boulder, Colo., Westview Press, 1993.

Rotblat, J., ed., *Nuclear Weapons: The Road to Zero*, Westview Press, 1998.

Sagan, S. D. and Waltz, K. N., *The Spread of Nuclear Weapons. A Debate*, New York and London, W. W. Norton and Co., 1995.

Schneider, B. R. and Dowdy, W. L., eds, *Pulling Back from the Brink: Reducing and Countering Nuclear Threats*, London, Frank Cass, 1998.

Simpson, J. and Howlett, D. eds, *The Future of the Non-Proliferation Treaty*, London, Macmillan, 1995.

Spector, L. S. and McDonough, M. G. with Medeiros, E. S., *Tracking Nuclear Proliferation 1995*, Washington, DC, Carnegie Endowment for International Peace, 1995.

Stansfield Turner, R., *Caging the Nuclear Genie: An American Challenge for Global Security*, Boulder, Colo., Westview Press, 1997.

Sur, Serge, ed., *Disarmament and Arms Limitation Obligations: Problems of Compliance and Enforcement*, Aldershot, Hants, Dartmouth for UNIDIR, 1994, p. 8.

Articles, chapters and other documents

Ahmed, S., 'Pakistan's Nuclear Weapons Programme: Turning Points and Nuclear Choices', *International Security*, Vol. 23, No. 4, Spring 1999, pp. 178–204.

Alpher, J., 'Israel's security concerns in the peace process', *International Affairs*, Vol. 70, No. 2, April 1994, pp. 229–41.

Andreani, G., 'The Disarray of US Non-Proliferation Policy', *Survival*, Vol. 41, No. 4, Winter 1999–2000, pp. 42–61.

Arnett, Eric, 'The Primacy of Politics: Cooperative versus Confrontational Approaches to Compliance', in James Brown, ed., *New Horizons and New Strategies in Arms Control*, Albuquerque, N. Mex., Sandia National Laboratories, 1998, pp. 331–52.

Arquilla, J. and Karmel, S. M., 'Welcome to the Revolution ... on Chinese Military Affairs', *Defense Analysis*, Vol. 13, No. 3, December 1997, pp. 255–70.

Ayoob, M., 'The Security Problematic of the Third World', *World Politics*, Vol. 43, January 1993, pp. 257–83.

Ayoob, M., 'The New-Old Disorder in the Third World', *Global Governance*, Vol. 1, No. 1, Winter 1995, pp. 59–77.

Bailey, K., 'Responding to the Threat of Biological Weapons', *Security Dialogue*, Vol. 26, No. 4, 1995, pp. 383–97.

Bailey, K., 'Reversing Missile Proliferation', *Orbis*, Vol. 35, No. 1, Winter 1991, pp. 5–14.

Banerjee, D., 'Revolution in Military Affairs', *Journal of the United Services Institute of India*, Vol. CXXVII, July–September 1997, pp. 299–309.

Batsanov, S., 'Practical Aspects Concerning the Implementation of the Convention Prohibiting Chemical Weapons', *Disarmament*, Vol. XVI, No. 3, 1993, pp. 123–40.

Belous, V., 'Key Aspects of the Russian Nuclear Strategy', *Security Dialogue*, Vol. 28, No. 2, June 1997, pp. 159–71.

Benson, S., 'Competing Views on Strategic Arms Reduction', *Orbis*, Vol. 42, No. 4, Fall 1998, pp. 587–604.

Betts, R. K., 'The New Threat of Mass Destruction', *Foreign Affairs*, Vol. 77, No. 1, January–February 1998, pp. 26–42.

Blair, B. G., Feiveson, H. A. and von Hippel, F., 'Taking Nuclear

Weapons Off Hair-Trigger Alert', *Scientific American*, November 1997, pp. 42–9.

Bluth, C., 'Strategic Nuclear Weapons and US–Russian Relations: From Confrontation to Co-operative Denuclearization?', *Contemporary Security Policy*, Vol. 15, No. 1, April 1994, pp. 80–109.

Brooks, L., 'START: An End and a Beginning', *Disarmament*, Vol. XV, No. 2, 1992, pp. 9–18.

Brown, C., 'Really-existing Liberalism and International Order', *Millennium*, Vol. 23, No. 3, Winter 1992, pp. 313–28.

Brown, H., 'Transatlantic Security in the Pacific Century', *The Washington Quarterly*, Vol. 18, No. 4, Autumn 1995, pp. 77–86.

Brown, M. E., *Phased Nuclear Disarmament and US Defense Policy*, Occasional Paper No. 30, The Henry L. Stimson Center, Washington, DC, October 1996.

Bunn, G., 'The Status of Norms Against Nuclear Testing', *The Nonproliferation Review*, Vol. 6, No. 2, Winter 1999, pp. 20–32.

Buzan, B., 'New Patterns of Global Security in the Twenty-first Century', *International Affairs*, Vol. 67, No. 3, July 1991, pp. 431–51.

Cambone, S. A. and Garrity, P. J., 'The Future of US Nuclear Policy', *Survival*, Vol. 36, No. 4, Winter 1994–95, pp. 73–95.

Carter, A., Deutch, J. and Zelikow, P., 'Catastrophic Terrorism: Tackling the New Danger', *Foreign Affairs*, Vol. 77, No. 6, November–December 1998, pp. 80–94.

Chase, R. S., Hill, E. B. and Kennedy, P., 'Pivotal States and U. S. Strategy', *Foreign Affairs*, Vol. 75, No. 1, January–February 1996, pp. 33–51.

Chayes, A. and Chayes, A. H., 'On compliance', *International Organization*, Vol. 47, No. 2, Spring 1993, pp. 175–205.

Chellany, B., 'The Challenge of Nuclear Arms Control in South Asia', *Survival*, Vol. 35, No. 3, Autumn 1993, pp. 121–36.

Cohen, A., 'The Nuclear Equation in a New Middle East', *The Nonproliferation Review*, Vol. 2, No. 2, Winter 1995, pp. 12–30.

Cohen, A. and Pilat, J. F., 'Assessing Virtual Nuclear Arsenals', *Survival*, Vol. 40, No. 1, Spring 1998, pp. 129–144.

Committee on Nuclear Policy, *Jump-START: Retaking the Initiative to Reduce Post-Cold War Nuclear Dangers*, The Henry L. Stimson Center, Washington, DC, February 1999.

Daalder, I. H., Goldgeier, J. M. and Lindsay, J. M., 'Deploying NMD: Not Whether, But How', *Survival*, Vol. 42, No. 1, Spring 2000, pp. 6–28.

Dean, J., 'Neutralizing Nuclear Weapons', *The Washington Quarterly*, Vol. 17, No. 4, Autumn 1994, pp. 31–52.

Deep Cuts Study Group, *A Strategy of Staged Reductions and De-alerting of Nuclear Forces*, Princeton University, 1996.

Delpech, T., 'What Future for Nuclear Weapons?', *Security Dialogue*, Vol. 25, No. 4, December 1994, pp. 405–8.

Downs, G. W., Rocke, D. M. and Barsoom, P. N., 'Is the Good News About Compliance Good News About Cooperation?', *International Organization*, Vol. 50, No. 3, Summer 1996, pp. 379–406.

Doyle, M., 'Kant, Liberal Legacies and Foreign Affairs', Part 1, *Philosophy and Public Affairs*, Vol. 12, No. 3, 1983, pp. 323–53.

Doyle, M., 'Kant, Liberal Legacies and Foreign Affairs', Part 2, *Philosophy and Public Affairs*, Vol. 12, No. 4, 1983, pp. 204–35.

Eban, A., 'The U. N. Idea Revisited', *Foreign Affairs*, Vol. 74, No. 5, September–October 1995, pp. 39–55.

Eberstadt, N., 'Population Change and National Security', *Foreign Affairs*, Vol. 70, No. 3, Summer 1991, pp. 115–31.

Edmonds, M., 'British Army 2000 External Influences on Force Design', *The Occasional*, No. 21, Strategic and Combat Studies Institute UK, 1996.

Ehsan Ahrari, M., 'Growing Strong: The Nuclear Genie in South Asia', *Security Dialogue*, Vol. 30, No. 4, December 1999, pp. 431–44.

Facing Nuclear Dangers: An Action Plan for the 21st Century, Report of the Tokyo Forum for Nuclear Non-Proliferation and Disarmament, 25 July 1999, http://www. mofa. go. jp/policy/un/disarmament/forum/tokyo9907/key. html.

Falkenrath, R., 'Confronting Nuclear, Biological and Chemical Terrorism', *Survival*, Autumn 1998, Vol. 40, No. 3, pp. 43–65.

Feiveson, H. and von Hippel, F., 'Beyond START: How to Make Much Deeper Cuts', *International Security*, Vol. 15, No. 1, Summer 1990, pp. 154–80.

Ferguson, C., 'Sparking a Buildup: U. S. Missile Defense and China's Nuclear Arsenal', *Arms Control Today*, March 2000.

115

Fetter, S., 'Ballistic Missiles and Weapons of Mass Destruction: What Is the Threat? What Should be Done?', *International Security*, Vol. 16, No. 1, Summer 1991, pp. 5–42.

Fetter, S., *Verifying Nuclear Disarmament*, Occasional Paper No. 29, The Henry L. Stimson Center, Washington, DC, October 1996.

Findlay, T., *The Verification and Compliance Regime for a Nuclear Weapon-Free World*, ISIS Briefing Paper 199.

Fisher, C., *Reformation and Resistance: Nongovernmental Organizations and the Future of Nuclear Weapons*, Report No. 29, The Henry L. Stimson Center, Washington, DC, May 1999.

Freedman, L., 'Great Powers, Vital Interests and Nuclear Weapons', *Survival*, Vol. 36, No. 4, Winter 1994–95, pp. 52–72.

Freedman, L., 'Britain and the Revolution in Military Affairs', *Defense Analysis*, Vol. 14, No. 1, April 1998, pp. 55–66.

Ganguly, S., 'India's Pathway to Pokhran II: The Prospects and Sources on New Delhi's Nuclear Weapons Programme', *International Security*, Vol. 23, No. 4, Spring 1999, pp. 148–77.

Ganguly, S., *Emergent Security Issues in South Asia*, Director's Series on Proliferation, No. 8, Lawrence Livermore National Laboratory, 1995, pp. 23–32.

Gates, S., Knutsen, T. L. and Moses, J. W., 'Democracy and Peace: A More Sceptical View', *Journal of Peace Research*, Vol. 33, February 1996, pp. 1–10.

Glaser, C., 'The Flawed Case for Nuclear Disarmament', *Survival*, Vol. 40, No. 1, Spring 1998, pp. 112–28.

Grand, C., *A French Nuclear Exception*, Occasional Paper No. 38, The Henry L. Stimson Center, Washington, DC, January 1998.

Gronlund, L. and Lewis, G., 'How a Limited National Missile Defense Would Impact on the ABM Treaty', *Arms Control Today*, Vol. 29, No. 7, November 1999, pp. 7–13.

Hagerty, D., 'Nuclear Deterrence in South Asia: The 1990 Indo-Pakistan Crisis', *International Security*, Vol. 20, No. 3, Winter 1995–96, pp. 79–114.

Halperin, M., 'Defining "Eliminating" Nuclear Weapons', *Disarmament Diplomacy*, No. 19, October 1997, pp. 5–6.

116

Harvey, J. and Rubin, U., 'Controlling Ballistic Missiles: How Important? How To Do It?', *Arms Control Today*, Vol. 22, No. 2, March 1992, pp. 13–18.

Helman, U., 'Sustainable Development: Strategies for Reconciling Environment and Economy in the Developing World', *The Washington Quarterly*, Vol. 18, No. 4, Autumn 1995, pp. 189–207.

Herby, P., 'Building the Chemical Disarmament Regime', *Arms Control Today*, Vol. 23, No. 7, September 1993, pp. 14–19.

Howlett, D. and Simpson, J., 'Nuclear Proliferation: The Evolving Policy Debate', *Contemporary Security Policy*, Vol. 20, No. 3, December 1999, pp. 198–230.

Huaqiu, L., *Steps Towards A Nuclear Weapon Free World*, Current Decisions Reports No. 18, Oxford Research Group, July 1997.

Huntington, S., 'The Clash of Civilizations', *Foreign Affairs*, Vol. 72, No. 3, Summer 1993, pp. 22–49.

Ibrügger, L., *The Revolution in Military Affairs*, Reports Adopted in 1998, Science and Technology Committee, North Atlantic Assembly, International Secretariat, Brussels, November 1998.

Ibrügger, L., *The South Asian Nuclear Crisis and the Future of Non-Proliferation Policies*, Reports Adopted in 1998, Science and Technology Committee, North Atlantic Assembly, International Secretariat, Brussels, November 1998.

Iklé, F. C., 'After Detection, What?', *Foreign Affairs*, Vol. 39, Fall 1961, p. 208.

Iklé, F. C., 'The Second Coming of the Nuclear Age', *Foreign Affairs*, Vol. 75, No. 1, January–February 1996, pp. 119–28.

'Is Arms Control Dead?', special section, *The Washington Quarterly*, Vol. 23, No. 2, Spring 2000, pp. 171–231. Contributions by H. Brown, J. Schlesinger, T. Graham, J. Steinbruner, S. Cambone and B. Roberts.

Jervis, R., 'Cooperation Under the Security Dilemma', *World Politics*, Vol. 30, No. 2, 1978, pp. 167–214.

Jervis, R., 'Security Regimes', *International Organization*, Vol. 36, No. 2, Spring 1982, pp. 357–78.

Joeck, N., *Maintaining Nuclear Stability in South Asia*, Adelphi Paper 312, International Institute for Strategic Studies, 1997.

Johnson, R., *British Perspectives on the Future of Nuclear Weapons*, Occasional Paper No. 37, The Henry L. Stimson Center, Washington, DC, January 1998.

Johnston, A. I., 'China's New "Old Thinking": The Concept of Limited Deterrence', *International Security*, Vol. 20, No. 3, Winter 1995–6, pp. 5–42.

Joseph, R. G. and Reichart, J. F., 'The Case for Nuclear Deterrence Today', *Orbis*, Winter 1998, pp. 7–19.

Junnola, J., 'Conflict Avoidance and Confidence Building in the Middle East', in Junnola J. and Krepon M., eds, *Regional Confidence Building in 1995: South Asia, the Middle East, and Latin America, Report No. 20*, December 1995, pp. 11–36.

Kamp, K. H., 'The Relevance of Nuclear Weapons in NATO', *Defense Analysis*, Vol. 15, No. 3, pp. 293–304.

Karl, D. J., 'Proliferation Pessimism and Emerging Nuclear Powers', *International Security*, Vol. 21, No. 3, Winter 1996–97, pp. 87–119.

Karp, A., 'The New Politics of Missile Proliferation', *Arms Control Today*, Vol. 26, No. 8, October 1996, pp. 10–14.

Keller, A., 'Assessing the First Year of the CWC', *The Nonproliferation Review*, Vol. 5, No. 3, Spring–Summer 1998, pp. 27–35.

Kennedy, P. and Russett, B., 'Reforming the United Nations', *Foreign Affairs*, Vol. 74, No. 5, September–October 1995, pp. 56–71.

Koblentz, G., 'Theatre Missile Defense and South Asia: A Volatile Mix', *The Nonproliferation Review*, Vol. 4, No. 3, Spring–Summer 1997, pp. 54–62.

Kortunov, S., 'Russian Deterrent Forces in the Post-Cold War Environment', *Disarmament*, Vol. XV, No. 3, 1992, pp. 1–17.

Lacey, E., 'Tackling the Biological Weapons Threat: The Next Proliferation Challenge', *The Washington Quarterly*, Vol. 17, No. 4, Autumn 1994, pp. 53–64.

Lake, D., 'Powerful Pacifists: Democratic States and War', *American Political Science Review*, Vol. 86, No. 1, March 1992, pp. 24–37.

Layne, C., 'Kant or Cant. The Myth of the Democratic Peace', *International Security*, Vol. 19, No. 2, Fall 1994, pp. 5–49.

Lee, S. J. and Sheehan, M., 'Building Confidence and Security on the Korean Peninsula', *Contemporary Security Policy*, Vol. 16, No. 3, December 1995, pp. 267–98.

Legro, J. W., 'Which Norms Matter?', *International Organization*, Winter 1997, Vol. 51, No. 1, pp. 31–63.

Leonard, J., 'Steps Toward a Middle East Free of Nuclear Weapons', *Arms Control Today*, Vol. 21, No. 3, April 1991, pp. 10–14.

Levy, M. A., 'Is the Environment a National Security Issue?', *International Security*, Vol. 20, No. 2, Fall 1995, pp. 35–62.

Makinda, S., 'Sovereignty and Global Security', *Security Dialogue*, Vol. 29, No. 3, September 1998, pp. 281–92.

Manning, R., 'The Nuclear Age: The Next Chapter', *Foreign Policy*, No. 109, Winter 1997–98, pp. 70–84.

Mathews, J. T., 'Redefining Security', *Foreign Affairs*, Vol. 68, No. 2, Spring 1989, pp. 162–77.

Matthews, R. and McCormack, T., 'Prevention is Better than Cure: Pre-empting Inspection-related Disputes under the Chemical Weapons Convention', *Contemporary Security Policy*, Vol. 16, No. 3, December 1995, pp. 396–420.

May, M., 'Nuclear Weapons in the New World Order', *Disarmament*, Vol. XV, No. 3, 1992, pp. 18–45.

Mazarr, M. J., 'Virtual Nuclear Arsenals', *Survival*, Vol. 37, No. 3, Autumn 1995, pp. 7–26.

MccGwire, M., 'Is There a Future for Nuclear Weapons?', *International Affairs*, Vol. 70, No. 2, April 1994, pp. 211–28.

Mearsheimer, J., 'Back to the Future: Instability in Europe After the Cold War', *International Security*, Vol. 15, No. 1, Summer 1990, pp. 5–56.

Mendelsohn, J., 'START II and Beyond', *Arms Control Today*, Vol. 26, No. 8, October 1996, pp. 3–7.

Mitchell, R. B, 'International Control of Nuclear Proliferation: Beyond Carrots and Sticks', *The Nonproliferation Review*, Vol. 5, No. 1, Fall 1997, pp. 40–50.

Moltz, J. C., 'Missile Proliferation in East Asia: Arms Control vs. TMD Responses', *The Nonproliferation Review*, Vol. 4, No. 3, Spring–Summer 1997, pp. 63–71.

Müller, H., 'Neither Hype Nor Complacency: WMD Proliferation after the Cold War', *The Nonproliferation Review*, Vol. 4, No. 2, Winter 1997, pp. 62–71.

Nadelmann, E., 'Global Prohibition Regimes: The Evolution of Norms in International Society', *International Organization*, Vol. 44, No. 4, Autumn 1990, pp. 479–526.

Nazarkin, Y., 'Strategic Nuclear Disarmament in a New Era', *Disarmament*, Vol. XV, No. 2, 1992, pp. 19–31.

Nye, J. S., 'Arms Control After the Cold War', *Foreign Affairs*, Vol. 68, No. 5, Winter 1989–90, pp. 42–64.

Ogilvie-White, T., 'Is There a Theory of Nuclear Proliferation? An Analysis of the Contemporary Debate', *The Nonproliferation Review*, Vol. 4, No. 1, Fall 1996, pp. 43–60.

O'Neill, R., 'Britain and the Future of Nuclear Weapons', *International Affairs*, Vol. 71, No. 4, October 1995, pp. 747–61.

Ould-Mey, M., 'Global Adjustment: Implications for Peripheral States', *Third World Quarterly*, Vol. 15, No. 2, 1994, pp. 319–36.

Ozga, D. A., 'Back to Basics on the NPT Review Process', *Security Dialogue*, Vol. 31, No. 1, March 2000, pp. 41–54.

Panofsky, W. K. H., 'Dismantling the Concept of "Weapons of Mass Destruction"', *Arms Control Today*, Vol. 28, No. 3, April 1998, pp. 3–8.

Park, M., '"Lure" North Korea', *Foreign Policy*, No. 97, Winter 1994–95, pp. 97–105.

Paul, T. V., 'Nuclear Taboo and War Initiation in Regional Conflicts', *Journal of Conflict Resolution*, Vol. 39, No. 4, December 1995, pp. 696–718.

Paul, T. V., 'The Paradox of Power: Nuclear Weapons in a Changing World', *Alternatives*, Vol. 20, No. 4, October–December 1995, pp. 479–500.

Pearson, G., 'The BWTC Protocol Enters the Endgame', *Disarmament Diplomacy*, No. 39, July–August 1999, pp. 6–13.

Preventing Deadly Conflict, Carnegie Corporation of New York, December 1997.

Quinlan, M., 'The Future of Nuclear Weapons: Policy for Western Possessors', *International Affairs*, Vol. 69, No. 3, July 1993, pp. 485–96.

Quinlan, M., *Thinking About Nuclear Weapons*, RUSI Whitehall Paper No. 41, 1997.

Rathjens, G., 'Rethinking Nuclear Proliferation', *The Washington Quarterly*, Winter 1995, Vol. 18, No. 1, pp. 107–22.

Report of the Canberra Commission on the Elimination of Nuclear Weapons, Australian Department of Foreign Affairs and Trade, 1996.

Rinne, R. L., *An Alternative Framework for the Control of Nuclear Materials*, CISAC, Stanford University, May 1999.

Roberts, A., 'The United Nations and International Security', *Survival*, Vol. 35, No. 2, Summer 1993, pp. 3–30.

Roberts, B., 'From Nonproliferation to Antiproliferation', *International Security*, Vol. 18, No. 1, Summer 1993, pp. 139–73.

Roberts, B., *Chemical Disarmament and International Security*, Adelphi Paper 267, International Institute for Strategic Studies, Spring 1992.

Robinson, C. P. and Bailey, K., 'To Zero or Not to Zero: A US Perspective on Nuclear Disarmament', *Security Dialogue*, Vol. 28, No. 2, June 1997, pp. 149–58.

Rogers, P., 'Responding to Western Intervention – Conventional and Unconventional Options', *Defense Analysis*, Vol. 14, No. 1, April 1998, pp. 41–54.

Rubin, U., 'How Much Does Ballistic Missile Proliferation Matter?', *Orbis*, Vol. 35, No. 1, Winter 1991, pp. 29–39.

Sagan, S. D., 'The Perils of Proliferation', *International Security*, Vol. 18, No. 4, Spring 1994, pp. 66–107.

Sagan, S. D., 'Three Theories in Search of a Bomb', *International Security*, Vol. 21, No. 3, Winter 1996–97, pp. 54–86.

Sagan, S. D., 'The Commitment Trap: Why the United States Should Not Use Nuclear Threats to Deter Biological and Chemical Weapons Attacks', *International Security*, Vol. 24, No. 4, Spring 2000, pp. 85–115.

Sanders, B., 'The 1995 NPT Review and Extension Conference: An Overview', *Contemporary Security Policy*, Vol. 16, No. 3, December 1995, pp. 421–8.

Schell, J., 'The Abolition', *The New Yorker*, 1984 reprinted in *The Washington Quarterly*, Vol. 20, No. 3, Summer 1997, pp. 143–52.

Schweller, R., 'Domestic Structure and Preventive War: Are Democracies More Pacific?', *World Politics*, Vol. 44, No. 2,

January 1992, pp. 235–69.

Shambaugh, D., 'China's Military Views the World: Ambivalent Security', *International Security*, Vol. 24, No. 3, Winter 1999–2000, pp. 52–79.

Smithson, A., 'Implementing the Chemical Weapons Convention', *Survival*, Vol. 36, No. 1, Spring 1994, pp. 80–95.

Sokov, N., 'Russia's Strategic Potential in the Year 2010', *International Affairs* (Moscow), Vol. 44, No. 5, 1998, pp. 127–40.

Spector, L. S., 'Neo-Nonproliferation', *Survival*, Vol. 37, No. 1, Spring 1995, pp. 66–85.

Srivastava, A., 'A Russian Re-Evaluation of the ABM Treaty? Implications for US-Russian Relations and Arms Control in Asia', *Disarmament Diplomacy*, No. 39, July–August 1999, pp. 2–5.

Stansfield Turner, R., 'The Specter of Nuclear Proliferation', *Security Dialogue*, Vol. 29, No. 3, September 1998, pp. 293–301.

Steinberg, G., 'Middle East Arms Control and Regional Security', *Survival*, Vol. 36, No. 1, Spring 1994, pp. 126–41.

Steinberg, G., 'Middle East Peace and the NPT Extension Decision', *The Nonproliferation Review*, Vol. 4, No. 1, Fall 1996, pp. 17–29.

Steinbruner, J., 'Biological Weapons: A Plague Upon All Houses', *Foreign Policy*, No. 109, Winter 1997–98, pp. 85–112.

Steinbruner, J., 'National Missile Defense: Collision in Progress', *Arms Control Today*, Vol. 29, No. 7, November 1999, pp. 3–13.

Subrahmanyam, K., 'Paths to Nuclear Disarmament', *USI Journal*, New Delhi, Vol. CXXIII, April–June 1993, pp. 205–15.

Telp, C., 'Theatre Missile Defense and US Security in South Asia', *Defense Analysis*, Vol. 15, No. 1, 1999, pp. 63–78.

Thakur, R., 'Envisioning Nuclear Futures', *Security Dialogue*, Vol. 31, No. 1, March 2000, pp. 25–40.

Thayer, B., 'The Causes of Nuclear Proliferation and the Utility of the Nuclear Nonproliferation Regime', *Security Studies*, Vol. 4, No. 3, Spring 1995, pp. 463–519.

Thomas, C., 'New Directions in Thinking About Security in the Third World', in K. Booth, ed., *New Thinking About Strategy and International Security*, HarperCollins, pp. 267–89.

Tucker, J., 'Strengthening the BWC: Moving Towards a Compliance Protocol', *Arms Control Today*, Vol. 28, No. 1, January–February 1998, pp. 20–27.

Utgoff, V., *Nuclear Weapons and the Deterrence of Biological and Chemical Warfare*, Occasional Paper No. 36, The Henry L. Stimson Center, Washington, DC, October 1997.

Walker, R., 'Nuclear Disarmament: Zero and How To Get There', *Security Dialogue*, Vol. 28, No. 2, June 1997, pp. 137–47.

Walker, W., 'The Risks of Further Nuclear Testing in South Asia', *Arms Control Today*, Vol. 29, No. 6, September–October 1999, pp. 20–25.

Walker, W., 'India's Nuclear Labyrinth', *The Nonproliferation Review*, Vol. 4, No. 1, Fall 1996, pp. 61–77.

Wallander, C. A., 'Wary of the West: Russian Security Policy at the Millennium', *Arms Control Today*, March 2000, http://www.armscontrol.org/ACT/march00/cwmr.00htm.

Waltz, K. N., 'Nuclear Myths and Political Realities', *American Political Science Review*, Vol. 84, No. 3, September 1990.

Wilkening, D. A., 'The Future of Russia's Strategic Nuclear Force', *Survival*, Vol. 40, No. 3, Autumn 1998, pp. 89–111.

Wilkening, D. A., 'Amending the ABM Treaty', *Survival*, Vol. 42, No. 1, Spring 2000, pp. 29–45.

Williams, P., 'Nuclear Weapons and Arms Control', Chapter 8 in J. Baylis and N. Rengger, eds, *Dilemmas of World Politics*, Clarendon Press, Oxford, 1992, pp. 205–27.

Witney, N. K. J., 'British Nuclear Policy After the Cold War', *Survival*, Vol. 36, No. 4, Winter 1994–95, pp. 96–112.

Yasmeen, S. and Dixit, A., *Confidence-building in South Asia*, Occasional Paper No. 23, The Henry L. Stimson Center, Washington, DC, September 1995.

Yost, D. S., 'Nuclear Debates in France', *Survival*, Vol. 36, No. 4, Winter 1994–95, pp. 113–39.

Zanders, J. P., 'Assessing the Risk of Chemical and Biological Weapons Proliferation to Terrorists', *The Nonproliferation Review*, Vol. 6, No. 4, Fall 1999, pp. 17–34.

Zukang, S., 'US National Missile Defense Plans', *Disarmament Diplomacy*, No. 43, January–February 2000, pp. 3–6.

Zuwei, H., 'START III and Beyond', *AGNI: Studies in International Strategic Issues* (Journal of the Forum for Strategic and Security Studies, New Delhi), Vol. 3, No. 1, June–September 1997, pp. 10–11.